NORTHSTAR

Cocktails

JOHNNY MICHAELS

★ AND ★

THE NORTH STAR BARTENDERS' GUILD

All royalties from the sale of this book will benefit the animal welfare organization SPCA International.

Borealis Books is an imprint of the Minnesota Historical Society Press.

www.mhspress.org

Unless otherwise noted, all photography is by Kate N. G. Sommers.

The Minnesota Historical Society Press is a member of the Association of American University Presses.

Manufactured in Canada.

10 9 8 7 6 5 4 3 2 1

♾ The paper used in this publication meets the minimum requirements of the American National Standard for Information Sciences—Permanence for Printed Library Materials, ANSI Z39.48–1984.

International Standard Book Number
ISBN: 978-0-87351-837-6 (cloth)
ISBN: 978-1-68134-070-8 (paper)

Library of Congress Cataloging-in-Publication Data

Michaels, Johnny.
    North Star cocktails / Johnny Michaels and the North Star Bartenders' Guild.
       p.   cm.
    ISBN 978-0-87351-837-6 (hardback)
    1. Cocktails.   2. Cookbooks.   I. North Star Bartenders' Guild.   II. Title.
    TX951.M527   2011
    641.87′4—dc23   2011032925

Contents

Sermon on the Bar

The following thoughts and viewpoints are those of Johnny Michaels and do not represent those of the North Star Bartenders' Guild.

For Brutus, Lucy, and Brando

My fellow Americans, people of the Earth planet, my name is Johnny Michaels, and I'm a DrinkMaker. I can execute classic cocktails (some, anyway) and also create originals (even if most of them are really just variations of, or rebranded, classics). Most people refer to me and others like myself as *mixologists*, but it's never been a term I've cared for. It seems too clinical and scientific to me. We don't call chefs *cookologists*, do we? I call them *FoodCookers*, for fun, because it's always fun joking around with the kitchen staff. With my looks and personality, I should've been a cook. But the way I see it, I make drinks, so I'm a DrinkMaker.

One summer back in the day, I was an ice cream man, and now I like to think of myself as an ice cream man for big kids, being a bartender. I make the treats, as well as serve them up, but if you really think about what we do, what we are, we're really stewards of people's good times. Everyone works hard at their jobs, and then come the pressures and obligations of everyday life, families, girlfriends, boyfriends, exes, car trouble, snow emergencies, falling anvils, and what have you. People often get to show themselves a good time only once a week (if that), which is why it's such an honor when they choose to visit us instead of doing something else.

Our guests are choosing quality over quantity, to celebrate life instead of getting drunk. That's the first lesson I give my barbacks. I try to make sure they understand what it's really all about before they invest themselves, and if they're barbacking for me, they WILL invest themselves. They're like the marines of the restaurant world. I usually try to talk them out of it for at least an hour, to see why and how bad they want the job. If you want to bartend, you need to do it for the love of the game. People like to think bartending is all socializing, smiling, flirting, crafting cocktails, and collecting a bunch of money. But working behind a busy bar is like being in a boat in a stormy sea, leaks popping faster than you can plug them—and when the bullets fly, don't forget to smile.

If you're just after money, be a server. They're last in, first out, and make more than we do. If you want to bartend, you better really love the physical act of making cocktails with your hands, serving people, and constantly racking your brain trying to think up new ideas, anything and everything to make people happy—to help them unwind, relax, smile, laugh. We serve good food and make the best drinks we can because in our business, if you really belong in it, we don't get off until our guests do. That's our contribution to society. We're some weird combination of psychiatrist, comedian, server, chef, philosopher, and glass washer. We might get paid with money, but we play this game to make people happy.

It's a tough job. We're bartending athletes, and we have to pay to play, prepare for every shift like it's going to be lights-out busy. We're on our feet eight to twelve hours and almost never stop moving. That's why we lead with the crowns of our helmets, why we drive people's thirst and aggravations into the turf, why we take it hard in the paint, why we throw and swing with everything we've got. We want to see people's eyes start twinkling, see that they are happy and the day's troubles are temporarily forgotten. The cooks, toiling away back in the kitchen, they don't get to see that. We do, but we pay a lot for our front-row seats. It's why we take performance-enhancing drugs before our games and painkillers after—even if I am only talking about espresso, ginseng, ibuprofen, and whiskey (wink, wink).

I remember way back when I first started bartending, almost twenty years ago, after three long years of barbacking, people would compliment me on my drinks, even simple ones like Gin and Tonics (and that's when you know you can shoot the ball), and I would tell them, "It's just like Jesus used to say, 'Make thy neighbor's drink as you would have thy neighbor make a drink for you.'" People never thought it was as funny as I did—like a lot of my jokes, I guess—but that's what it's really all about, no matter what you do. People can tell when you play the game that way even before they taste their drink.

It's never been a dream of mine to write a cocktail book. I buy them but don't read them. I was shocked when I was asked to do so by an organization as solid as the Minnesota Historical Society. I'm still fairly convinced my boss had something to do with it, figuring this was the only way to get me to write down the recipes so he could kick my pancakes out the door. I agreed to do it, but only if other members of our newly formed North Star Bartenders' Guild agreed to contribute recipes. Luckily for us, they did, so now you can get the recipes for some of your favorite Twin Cities' cocktails, from establishments past and present. After seeing their recipe contributions, I'm a bit embarrassed to show you some of mine, especially the ones from five-plus years ago, but you know what? People still ask for them, even when they haven't been on the menu for years. You can make them at home, serve them to your friends, and feel good knowing that you're helping out a bunch of helpless animals in the process. All North Star Bartenders' Guild events and projects are charity based, and all royalties from the sale of this book are going to the Society for the Prevention of Cruelty to Animals International. Thank you sincerely, and hope to see you soon.

Johnny Michaels

Tools and Tips

I tell people that making drinks is a lot like cooking, except with liquor. More like cooking than baking, in my opinion. A lot of the same rules apply, using high-quality ingredients and learning proper technique being the two main things. It also helps if you have the right tools for the job. As in cooking, you can do a lot of good stuff with a couple of well-chosen items: a good knife or two, a spoon, and a couple pots and pans. Some people like to have every gadget known to man crammed in their kitchens, and that's cool, too. Either route can be taken when outfitting your home bar, depending on what you want to do and what your style is.

Suggested Utensils and Equipment

Glassware. I love having a big selection of glasses. Different cocktails have their own personalities, and the correct glassware is crucial, like clothes on a person. Illustrations accompany each recipe in this book to give you an indication of the general size and shape of the ideal glass for each cocktail. Some of these glasses should be standard in a home bar, and others are for the enthusiast or advanced cocktail maker. I recommend having on hand, at bare minimum, martini glasses, collins glasses, rocks glasses, double rocks glasses, champagne flutes, and wineglasses. If you're into the vintage cocktail thing, buy some champagne coupes. Also, when reading the ingredients lists, think of the measurements as proportions. If you've got a bigger or smaller glass than the one used by the recipe's author, adjust accordingly.

Two shakers. There are two main styles, the Boston shaker, a large tin that fits over a clear pint glass or a smaller tin, and the cobbler shaker, a three-piece all-metal unit (I prefer the type with a raised lip around the strainer). I recommend both. It's like having one good pot and one good pan. You can do almost anything with them.

Tools of the trade

Hawthorn strainer. I prefer using a strainer over cracking open a two-piece Boston shaker, like an egg, and letting the liquid trickle out the open slit at the bottom. Unless people really master this technique, they frequently look clumsy doing it, are slow, and usually drop a rogue piece or two of ice in the glass. Hawthorn strainers fit over the top of a Boston shaker's tin or pint glass and have a spring-like strainer around half of their rim. Bartenders can adjust the pouring gap with their index finger and control things such as how much froth they want in their serving glass.

Fine-mesh/tea strainer. You want a smaller-width one that will fit atop a pint glass with a lightweight handle that won't cause the glass to tip over if you leave it unattended. Tea strainers are great when you're squeezing fresh juices with a citrus press and want to clarify the liquid as it goes into a jigger, or if you have powershaken a cocktail and want to catch the broken-off ice bits as you pour the drink. When a recipe calls for a cocktail to be "double strained," that means first by a Hawthorn strainer on a Boston tin and then through a tea strainer as it is poured into a glass.

The julep, Hawthorn, and fine-mesh tea strainers

A muddler or two. There are two main kinds of muddlers out there, metal and wood. I like the metal ones with the treaded, gripping footprint for muddling citrus in syrup. They grip the fruit and won't let it squirm away from you. I like the flat-bottomed wooden ones for mashing things, like peppers or fresh fruit. Make sure you pick a muddler that's long enough. Most of the time, you will be using a sturdy pint glass to muddle in, and it shocks me how many muddlers on the market are too short to do this without bruising your knuckles. You also want to select a muddler with a nice big and wide footprint. Skinnier ones will take longer to do the job and won't provide better results. Also, the top of the muddler should be comfortable and big enough to not bruise your palm in the event you ever make more than one drink at a time. I like OXO's metal muddler.

Two knives. You can spend as much or as little as you want on these. In fact, you probably own two suitable knives already. If you don't, put down this book and go to your nearest Asian food market. I've found they have great inexpensive straight-bladed knives (you don't want serrated knives). You want one 4-inch skinny-bladed, nimble knife for garnishes and such and one 8-inch thick-bladed knife (by "thick," I mean that the blade is taller from edge to top) for cutting lemons, limes, oranges, what-

Different muddler footprints

ever—just not your fingers. Citrus will dull your metal knives very quickly, so a knife sharpener is a great idea, too. For a couple of dollars, you can buy a sharpening stone, which takes some practice and skill to use, or go to a kitchen store and buy an easy-to-use one for around twenty dollars. Ceramic knives are another option. Citrus won't dull them, but they are more expansive and brittle, so be careful not to drop them.

Channel knife (twister). These are used to make citrus spirals and twists, so I call them *twisters* (like I said, I'm a DrinkMaker, the chefs are FoodCookers, and that channel knife is a twister). I recommend the OXO Good Grips brand. They're very sturdy and built to last, with a nice, thick cutting groove, which will make an easy-to-twist garnish (and no, I am not getting any kickbacks from OXO). Making twists takes some practice. It's a combination of hand strength and technique. Slow, powerful, and deliberate movements. Technique is more important than hand strength, and you'll be amazed at the importance of the fruit's cooperation. You'll soon become very picky when buying your lemons, oranges, and limes. You'll learn to look for certain traits in the fruit you pick. Some are great for juicing but can be very uncooperative when you try to skin them and vice versa. Room-temperature fruit also cooperates better than fruit straight out of the refrigerator: the peel is less likely to break when you try to spiral it with your fingers.

Cutting board. Wooden ones don't weather the storm of dishwashers very well, so that's something to consider. I've found those black synthetic slate types shred a bit after getting wet, and sometimes they leave little black bits on cut fruits. (I must be related to Inspector Clouseau, because it took me a while to figure that out.) Pretty much any kind will work fine. I have two, a large one I use when cutting lots of citrus before the shift and a smaller one I keep in my work area that I use when making *à la minute* garnishes.

Bar spoons. I don't use a bar spoon, so go ahead and stone me. If nobody liked them and never used them, I probably would. It is hard for me to use logic in defending my position on this, because they are cool and beautiful artistic tools, but I still don't like using them. They're good for stirring ice in a glass, spinning the twisted stem between your fingers to elegantly jostle the ice cubes around with the spoon paddle. You can measure out a bar spoon's worth of liqueurs or invert the spoon to layer liqueurs. They are handy. I just don't like using them.

I use inexpensive neon-green plastic chopsticks to stir things, or I just swirl things around in a Boston tin. A plastic straw will also give things a quick mix. It all depends on the situation: Are you taking your time at home making a nice cocktail for your friend after a hard day at work? Are you working in a fancy cocktail bar, where seating is limited and people expect to wait ten minutes or more for their drink? Are you laboring in a poorly designed bar in a high-volume lounge that tries to crank out craft cocktails as fast as humanly possible? Use whatever you like, though. I won't judge you on this one and hope you don't judge me. I just dig those chopsticks. I use a fresh, clean one for every drink.

Measured shot glass. I prefer these to jiggers, but that's just me. I free pour (I like to think I can shoot the ball, and I like to go fast) and don't use these very often unless I'm trying to document a recipe for something or other. A lot of jiggers are not clearly labeled, which is a huge aggravation for me. I hate poor design. I like using one nice,

Pedestrian plastic chopstick versus mighty bar spoon

clear utility shot glass with ounce, milliliter, teaspoon, and tablespoon measurements painted on the side of the glass. As for good jiggers, I recommend one of the newer metal models with rubber grips on the outside and multiple measuring lines grooved on the inside. You should most definitely use a jigger at home, for accuracy. I cannot argue with the fact that nobody, no matter how good they are, will free pour exactly all the time, but free pouring is faster than jiggering, and you can't have everything. I work in a high-volume bar disguised as a craft cocktail lounge, which is why I do a lot of premixing of several ingredients in the right proportions in one bottle for high-selling cocktails. It takes more prep work but is great for speed and accuracy. But you know what? I'm a pure scorer. Just give me the ball, and I'll nail the shot.

Metal pour spouts. Free pouring small, accurate amounts from liquor bottles, especially full and fancy ones that were designed to catch the eye but not pour cleanly or easily, is a hard thing to do for people who don't do it often. The use of pour spouts (I prefer the metal and rubber composites, not the neon plastic ones) will enable you to easily and accurately pour a quarter ounce whenever you want, without dripping expensive liquor everywhere and making a mess. If you don't like the way they look in your liquor collection, remove and rinse them after use and recap your bottles. If you leave the spouts in, it's also a good idea to get little rubber caps for them to keep out fruit flies.

Citrus press. I prefer squeezing individual wedges with my fingers. I know in my head how much juice I'm looking for, and it could be one, two, four, five pieces, depending on the fruit's quality. Lemons and limes come in different sizes, ripenesses (based on season and weather), and sugar contents (same). Recipes that call for the juice of half a lime are just too vague for my logic. I've seen a big, strong bartender crush every drop of juice out of his half lime while making a drink and, a minute later, a lazy, weak bartender, who's preoccupied with talking to coworkers and not putting any effort or care into what's being done, squeeze out only half as much juice. They are lucky I'm not their boss. Even if all bartenders are putting forth effort, the juice's sugar content and volume per lime will vary over the course of the year. So a citrus press is good to have, especially in conjunction with a small fine-mesh strainer. I recommend straining the juice into a glass and then measuring out how much you need. If the sweetness level needs adjustment, reach for your simple syrup or agave nectar. (The reason I use individual fruit pieces is because the bar I work at was not built for speed, so that's why I run and gun. Once a couple of bars designed by bartenders open and people see the difference it makes, this area will no longer be given second-class treatment by architects.)

Champagne stopper. People should drink more sparkling wine, because it's fun and sexy. (People love bubbles.) Having a good stopper means you can have as much or as little of a bottle as you want without committing to the whole thing. A stopper comes in extra handy when you use sparkling wine as a mixer in a cocktail, which, as you will see, I'm a big fan of.

Specialty ice tools: an ice pick, a hatchet, flexible silicone cubular (as in, like, totally cubular cubes, dude) ice trays, and even ice-ball molds. Ice is very important, as is understanding what ice does: chilling the liquid and diluting the ingredients. You can use different types of ice to achieve the same or very similar results, but you need to know how to use each kind properly. I shake each cocktail differently. First, I understand my drink and how I want my cocktail to turn out. Then I think about what ingredients are in it and what kind of ice is at my disposal, which will determine what kind of shaker I use and whether I shake or swirl it, how hard or gently, and for how long.

Some people love ice balls. They look cool and chill a drink really well with a minimal amount of dilution, but they generally take a day to make in a home freezer. (You can try to carve out an ice ball using an ice pick and knife but will probably injure yourself sooner or later.) Personally, I like rough-hewn, chopped or picked blocks of ice, which can be the same volume as a ball and, in my opinion, look cooler. I like the uniqueness of each one, especially if you take a big block of ice and expertly break it down with an ice pick. I guarantee it will go over at your next barbeque way better than pressing a button to fire up your new gas grill. You can also make a slab of ice with a deep-dish rectangular cake pan and then chop it up with a hatchet. You won't get the cubes that you can, after some practice, from an ice block, but it's pretty easy and less intimidating for some people than using an ice pick. Or, get in the habit of making a new ice ball every morning while you're making your coffee and then keep them in a bag in your freezer.

Squirt and eyedropper bottles. Many bartenders do not use squirt bottles, but to me they are indispensible. They don't look the prettiest, but if you're doing any volume or looking to go fast, you will want some. Just for things like salt solution or simple syrup, they are great. Kitchen or restaurant supply stores will usually carry them, and I'm sure they're available online. I like the semitransparent, semiopaque, wide-mouthed plastic models. They usually come in 12-, 24-, and 32-ounce sizes. I think the 32-ounce size is too big. The plastic is not thick enough to support a full bottle of liquid, and when you apply gentle squeezing pressure to pick up a full one, there's a good chance some will squirt out of it (embarrassing).

I also go to beauty supply stores and buy smaller plastic squirt bottles with long, fine-pointed dispensing nozzles. These are apparently used for dyeing hair, but I find they make precise dispensers for bitters and tinctures. (I got this idea from the Chefs, er, FoodCookers at La Belle Vie: they use these bottles to decorate plates with different flavored and colored oils and sauces.) They dispense very consistent amounts of liquid, regardless of whether the bottle is almost full or empty, something that is not true with commercially made bitters bottles.

Being a bartender requires a wide variety of skills. Not everyone has what I call a *wet thumb*, a natural touch, a shooter's touch, and not everyone is a great socializer. (I joke that they should have a velvet curtain for me, where I can just hand people drinks through an opening slit.) Nobody is great at everything. I've tried explaining to attractive, personable, dry-thumbed bartender trainees that a certain cocktail will take four shakes of a new Angostura bitters bottle and only one, maybe two, of an almost empty one. It just depends on how much comes out. They usually wrinkle and furrow their brows in a vain attempt to understand. You need to be in touch with what is coming out of your bottles, not just counting shakes. (The same is true with liquor and wine bottles: feel, don't count.)

Another option for bitters and finely controlled ingredients is the eyedropper bottle, which is great for precision but lousy for speed. For making cocktails at home, this is the way to go. If you're hosting an open-bar party for one hundred guests, maybe not. Beauty supply stores also sell great little affordable spray bottles, maybe holding three ounces, otherwise known as atomizers and selling for much more. They're great for misting the inside of a glass (say, absinthe for a Sazerac or vermouth for a Martini), as opposed to rinsing a glass with a small amount of liquid and dumping out the excess, and it takes about one-tenth the time. I've found that whatever you put in a bottle pretty much seasons it forever, so keep that in mind before spending a lot of money on one.

Wide-mouth mason jars. These jars are great for making infusions, bitters, tinctures, what have you. Label them with masking tape, so you don't need to buy new lids all the time. Why wide-mouth jars? Because I said so! Plus, they're easier to clean. And they don't retain odors the way plastic containers can. We're not canning with them, so the seal area's being larger isn't a disadvantage.

Pitchers, funnels, and measuring spoons. Cheap, useful, and handy. Want to save some money? Go to the dollar store and get a pitcher, a set of measuring spoons, and five different-sized funnels for three bucks. We bartenders like to make money, not waste it.

Cherry or olive pitter. One would be nice to have (works better on cherries than olives) but is not essential, especially if the fruit is to be muddled. A frugal person can carefully and safely remove a cherry pit with a two-dollar knife.

Blender. A blender is useful for making homemade ginger or fresh mint syrup. If you love cruise ship drinks, move this item up to the top of your list. The good news is that almost everyone has one, so if you ever want or need one, you probably won't have to buy one.

Large fine-mesh strainers or a chinois. These are very good to have when making syrups. A ladle is also helpful when straining things. You swirl and work it around the strainer and keep pressing until the mash is pretty dry. It's also good to have some cheesecloth or a linen napkin to more finely filter whatever you're making.

An expensive Büchner funnel can be bought if you get really serious about clarifying homemade bitters or liquids with powdery sediment. They are like big chemistry beakers with a side valve attached to a hand pump. The top of the beaker has a large rubber cork with a hole in it, into which a porcelain funnel/strainer fits. You also have to use special round-paper filters. You pump the air out of the beaker, which sucks the liquid in the funnel through the paper filter. These work well when time and gravity are not enough to filter something through a coffee filter inside a large *chinois* (a conical strainer with a metallic mesh).

If the liquid is thin enough, like an alcohol, and not thick and viscous, like simple syrup, I'll use the decanting method. Let all the powdery sediment sink to the bottom of the infusing bottle and then slowly pour off the top, clear liquid through a coffee strainer. Fit a linen napkin or some cheesecloth inside the chinois (making sure you dampen it first), pour in the bottom sludge, twist off the top of the napkin, and slowly squeeze, tightening and twisting until all the liquid has passed through and you're wringing a napkin with damp, powdery residue inside.

Lewis or canvas ice-crushing bag and mallet. Certain classic cocktails call for crushed ice. The canvas soaks up the meltage. The mallet also doubles as a great gavel for making proclamations.

Juice machine. These are great for creating new flavor combos from vegetables and some fruit but are bad for citrus fruits. They didn't use these before Prohibition, I'll tell you that.

Carbonator. This one is getting pretty out there . . . really. I like using them, but if you're all into classic cocktails and pre-Prohibition-style drinks, this is certainly something you don't need. Buy one if you like weird stuff as much as I do, though, and want to create new and psychedelic cocktails. I dig how you can buy a new one for only a hundred dollars. They're also great for making homemade nonalcoholic sodas. I use them to carbonate liquor when I want something to be intense. Club soda will water down a drink, and sometimes I want the potency *and* the bubbles. Legendary Replacements guitarist Bob Stinson once told me that if you want to get drunk fast, drink something hot or with bubbles. So I made him a hot drink with whiskey and sparkling cider. He wouldn't drink it.

Bartending Tips and Random Thoughts (as if I had any other kind)
I love it when young, aspiring bartenders ask me for advice. I like to tell them to be prepared to work while being extremely hung over and not to get their hopes up. The look on their faces is priceless! I then laugh and let them know I'm kidding and tell them what I'd tell anyone doing anything.

Do it because you love it, and work as hard as you can. If you think it's going to be all fun and easy, just a lot of smiling and gabbing and easy money, just forget it now and do yourself and any future employers a favor. Are you working your way through school or do you need a second job for some extra cash? Be a server. The hours are shorter, and the money is better. Bartend because you love it and would only daydream about it if you had a different job.

Classic cocktails are where it's at. Having said that, you will find little evidence of that in my recipes. I serve up what people order and seem to prefer at whatever restaurant I'm working for—different demos at different places. I'm always tracking their selections and tailoring my cocktail lists accordingly, and lately I am happy to report that classic cocktails are really starting to become popular out here in the Midwest. It is important to understand the mother recipes, the classic combinations, the ones first discovered because they were obvious mates.

Once you get a handle on that and the drink-making techniques required to execute them correctly, then you can start putting little twists and spins on things, creating "original" cocktails. True original cocktail ideas are getting harder to find every day, but I believe there are good ones still out there and tip my cap to people who toil trying to find them. For an example of this, check out Pip Hanson's Oliveto cocktail on p. 51. If I had only one piece of advice for you to keep in mind when making cocktails, it would be to strive for balance—not too sweet or dry, not too this or that, unless that is your intention. I love strong and bold flavors, but I love delicate and shy cocktails, too. They're just like songs and people. No one way is best.

To Jigger or Not to Jigger?

When it comes to actual bartending tips, or a philosophical discussion about technique, nothing comes to my mind more readily than the debate on whether to jigger or not to jigger (that and the ice factor). There is no logical argument against the jigger in an ideal world. All pro bartenders should be adept, fast, and comfortable using a jigger. The problem with jiggers is that almost no bars have been properly designed to accommodate their use in a high-volume setting.

Digital scales are another, even-more-accurate way to measure but, again, are hard to use while also being fast. I like to tell my barbacks and bartender trainees that they need to feel, be in touch with, what is coming out of their pour spouts. I think this is accomplished by feeling the microvibrations from the bubbling that

Different styles of jiggers

occurs with pour spouts. One just picks it up unconsciously over time. That's how it happened for me, but I think paying attention to it from the beginning will expedite the process. It's the same with pouring wine. If you're looking at the level rising in the glass, by the time you hit the brakes, you're going to overshoot your mark. Counting doesn't work either because sweeter liqueurs will slowly build up and eventually clog pour spouts.

Producing high-quality craft cocktails with speed is the next holy grail for the bartending and liquor industry. The top five percent of sophisticated cocktail drinkers will seek out and patiently wait for their drinks to be made with exacting precision, but there is another 50 percent of drinkers out there ripe for conversion, and I believe speed to be the missing unmet need for these people. If a popular signature cocktail requires smaller amounts of several liquors, liqueurs, and bitters, I see wisdom in premixing these ingredients to reduce a drink's production time.

I think pro bartenders should also be able to consistently nail easy shots, like 1-ounce pours, at a very high percentage rate. I admit that nobody, no matter how sweet a shooter's touch they possess, will always be 100 percent accurate, but simple pours can be executed at a very high success rate in bar settings that were not designed for speed.

The combination of using some premixed ingredients and jiggering is the happy medium. Once smart and wise architects, bartenders, and bar owners work together to design and build faster, more efficient bars, they will revolutionize the industry for the masses. Right now, there are too many kitchen managers who are being assigned the task of working with the architects during the design phase of new construction projects, and there's no way a chef will be able to design a better bar than a bartender. No offense to chefs—we're certainly not smarter than them—but we just know the intimacies of our jobs better. Bottom line, you should jigger at home, and that's that.

Shaking and Stirring

I like to compare the shaking of a cocktail to sautéing something. You need to know what product you're working with, what heat setting you've picked, and what kind of pan. I shake each drink differently, and sometimes the differences would appear minor to the observer, but the key is to be in tune with your ice, liquor type, and the cocktail you're making. Pick the proper shaker for the job, and focus on how you want the finished product to be. How frothy? How cold? How much water are you seeking to intentionally add? Factor everything together, and pay attention to what you're doing. The actual length of time of shaking, the amount and type of ice used, the motion, the power of the shake—everything is critical and should go into your mental equation. The same concepts apply to stirred cocktails. Are you stirring or swirling the liquor in a tin or in a pint glass? A pint glass will melt more ice than a tin will. The ice X factor is perhaps the trickiest part of drink making and requires the most finesse.

Homemade Ingredients

People assume that if something is homemade, it must be better than something produced in a factory. This is not always true. Some factories have been run by the same family for over a hundred years, and they will make a better, more cost-effective product than you ever will no matter how hard you try. Sometimes, a commercial producer will use certain varieties of fruit right after they're picked to make a syrup or frozen purée that has more flavor than the fruit varieties that have been chosen for their shipping durability and are over a week old by the time you get your hands on them. Fresh isn't always better. The same holds true for bitters and tinctures. Some things are worth the effort, and some are not. It's hard to beat Angostura bitters, but creating a new and unique flavor combo might be worth the effort. I like to use organic flavor extracts in some of my house-made syrups, but there is no cutting corners with mint or ginger syrup. There are only so many hours in the day (and night). Labor costs are a big factor, as is your free time. Pick your battles wisely. (I make some homemade syrups, infused liqueurs, tinctures, and bitters but also use some commercially available products.)

Bitters

Now, let's talk about the mysterious subject of bitters. Bitters are seasonings for a cocktail, used just like spices for food in the culinary world. Bitters are generally blends of different spice infusions, while tinctures are single flavor infusions. Bitters could use a branding makeover, since the term scares some people off. Not all bitters are even bitter. Before Prohibition, lots of varieties of bitters were available and, just like today, lots of bartenders made their own signature blends. You can too, but it's a lot of work and trial and error. Angostura, considered the king of bitters, was one of the only brands to survive Prohibition and is still awesome and hard to beat. Other brands I like are the Bitter Truth, Regan's Orange, Bittercube, and Peychaud's (the traditional bitters for a real Sazerac). It's just great that so many boutique bitters companies are producing all sorts of new flavors. Remember to think of them as you would spices: it's important to match the spice to the dish and to use the correct amount—less is usually more. You'll be surprised how quickly you'll love using them. They'll turn your cocktails from black and white to color to HD3D.

A Very Abbreviated
Twin Cities
Drinking History

Before getting into what's happening right now in the Twin Cities cocktail scene, it seems fitting to briefly touch on the history of cocktail and drinking culture in Minnesota. I have always figured that back in the day, people around here drank simple things like beer and whiskey, which turns out was pretty much the case. A lot of German immigrants settling in Minnesota and Wisconsin brought their beer-making skills with them (to the endless delight of future Packer fans). Farmers also converted large quantities of stored grain into smaller (but more fun and lucrative) stores of whiskey. Brandy was too expensive back then due to phylloxera insects' wiping out European grape crops. Domestic brandy didn't show up on the scene until the Korbel Brothers from California went to the World's Columbian Exposition in Chicago in 1893, and ever since then, this area has been one of the biggest brandy consumers in the country.

I remember hearing stories about lumberjacks and loggers working up in northern Minnesota, saving up some money, coming down the river to the Mill City, boozing it up until their money ran out, and then going back up north to work some more. Back then, bars would serve up free sandwiches and whatnot to get people to hang out and drink longer. Sounds like these early happy hours consisted of a loaf of bread sitting at the end of the bar, maybe with some slices of meat and cheese, really simple stuff.

My first restaurant job was at the historic Gluek's bar in Minneapolis, which was built in 1855. The Holcomb family has run and managed the bar since it reopened after Prohibition and now owns it. I don't think any other family has had as long a run as they have had at their location on Sixth Street. They are just cool, good people. They hired me off the street as a busboy. To help finance my short film projects, I needed a job with tip money, which really ended up being drinking money. I was just an Uptown kid back then, living day to day, barely getting by, and Lee Holcomb used to advance me small sums of money when I needed it. How many people would do that for their busboys? (I used to joke that I was a franchise busboy—ha!) I worked for them around ten years and am proud to have started off at such a historic place.

John Jahr Saloon, St. Paul, 1917

Right after Prohibition the bar was owned by the Gluek Brewing Company and was called Fransen's. It served Gluek's beer and shots of whiskey. I used to get blown away thinking about how many people had drank in that space over the years, of the countless human dramas that had unfolded in there. The place burned down, except the brick shell, in the 1980s, but they rebuilt it. Before the fire the building's top two floors each had twenty sleeping rooms and one bathroom, with the bar on the main floor. It was a workingman's bar and had been for a long time.

I had assumed that, back in the day, all the downtown bars were pretty much like this, but that was before I talked to Dean Phillips, president and CEO of Phillips Distilling Company and great-grandson of the founder, Jay Phillips. Dean has a treasure trove of local liquor artifacts, everything from pre-Prohibition unopened liquor bottles, recently discovered hidden behind a wall during a Kenwood-area home renovation, to a cocktail book titled *Good Things to Drink* (price: one dollar), written by Minneapolis bartender Frank Stutsman in 1909. It turns out that some places around here served drinks other than beer and whiskey back then.

Frank had worked in New York and Chicago before coming to Minneapolis, where he worked at Frank McCormack's Buffet Saloon and Chandler Brothers. The recipes are vintage for sure, calling for Tom gin (wasn't even called Old Tom yet, I guess), absinthe, Picon bitters, Italian vermouths, mint, fresh citrus juices, lots of egg whites, and even "young calf hoof jelly." Dean also has a huge collection of pictures of old bars and saloons. Some from before Prohibition had names like August Johnson's Saloon (Carver), Bueger Saloon (St. Paul), Carney Saloon (Mankato), Charles Lustig's Saloon (Stillwater), Edward Shelland Saloon (Minneapolis), Harris Saloon (Tenstrike), John Jahr Saloon (St. Paul), Kurtz's (Buffalo), the West Hotel (St. Paul), Matt Stayer's Saloon (Ely), Merchant's Saloon (Minneapolis), Donndelinger (St. Paul), and Sandell Bros Wholesale and Retail Liquor Dealers (St. Paul).

When Prohibition started, a lot of these bars turned into lunch counters and barely eked out a living selling sandwiches, soda pop, and bottled malt syrup, which had extremely low alcohol content. Others turned into speakeasies. The Hollyhocks Inn in St. Paul was an elegant one, with a private dining room on the main floor and even-more-private drinking rooms on the second and third floors. Apparently, this was the speakeasy of choice for local gangsters, so of course the socialites followed, and it became the place to be seen. A secret passageway led from the third floor to the basement, a getaway in the event of police raids.

After Prohibition, the beer flowed like wine, and so did the whiskey. It seems like the place to procure a good cocktail was at one of the nicer fine-dining restaurants, nightclubs, or hotels of the day. Schiek's (yeah, the strip club) has been around since before Prohibition and originally was a fine German restaurant. It has changed locations several times and has had different owners. It was a classy gentleman's club with nightly live music before turning into whatever it is today. The Casablanca nightclub, Whitestar, Freddy's, Charlie's, the very first Radisson Hotel (which had both the Viking Room and the Flame Room), the Leamington Hotel, the Hotel Ritz-Minnesotan, and the Haberdashery were all places one could find classic cocktails (Martinis, Manhattans, Old-Fashioneds, Daiquiris). In the 1950s the Nicollet Hotel shook things up with the introduction of the Waikiki Room and gave Minnesota its first taste of exotica, Polynesian tiki drinks. The original Nankin followed and offered other new and exciting tastes.

G & M Bar, Minneapolis, 1950

Gradually, things moved away from the classics, and the familiar, pedestrian mixed drinks I grew up with gained prominence. Luckily, there were still some bastions of quality where one could find a good cocktail, but they did not flourish. John Rimarcik acquired the Monte Carlo in 1985 and converted it from a working-man's bar into a fine-dining restaurant and classic cocktail bar, and it has carried that torch ever since. When I was younger and coming up through the ranks and another bartender and I would debate the proper way to serve a cocktail, I always ended the discussion by looking at my invisible WWMCD bracelet—What Would the Monte Carlo Do?—and that was that.

In the 1990s, some specialty drinks and cocktails started to appear here and there. They were usually way too sweet and designed to get women more intoxicated than they intended, which didn't help the cause. Slowly, some decent cocktail lists developed at places like Rainbow Chinese Restaurant, Palomino, Auriga, Azia, and Café Lurcat. I think the place that finally, really, got the Twin Cities going on the cocktail renaissance was the Town Talk Diner, opened in 2005 by Tim Niver and Aaron Johnson. Aaron's leadership and creativity behind the bar, plus a knowledge and skill set to execute proper classic cocktails, finally got the Twin Cities' attention, just as some of us were wondering if the cocktail revivals going on in bigger cities would ever make it here. I was lucky enough to be chosen to head up the cocktail program at La Belle Vie when it opened a few months later, and it's been on ever since.

New, great places are opening up all the time. It's a new golden age for great cocktails in the Twin Cities, and I'm sure it will work its way throughout the state. We might not have the rich cocktail history of some bigger cities, but if they know what's good for them, they should look out. (Minnesota is famous for our hot dish, also known as a casserole. Is a cocktail not a *cold dish*? Different ingredients mixed together in a synergistic way.) We are hard workers (hard-rock miners) and spend half the year cooped up indoors with nothing better to do than try to come up with new cocktails. In the NFL they call it *closing speed*, a cornerback's ability to close the gap between him and a wide receiver who has a step or two on him, and I'm seeing a lot of good young bartenders with some nice times in the forty. Objects in your rearview mirror may be closer than they appear . . .

Gin

	NAME	**The Music of Your Life**		
	SPIRIT	Gin	GLASS	Martini
	CREATOR	Johnny Michaels		

Let's start off with a modern-day, accepted version of a classic Martini. I dig the name. It's the slogan for an AM radio station that plays a lot of old-time music that I love. Speaking of things I love, I love gin, and you should, too. If you think you don't, well you just haven't dated the right people. If you're new to gin, I suggest starting off with Bombay Sapphire or one of the newer, softer styles inspired by it. Ask the best bartender you know for advice when it's not prime-time rush hour. You could also ease yourself into the gin pool by going half vodka, half gin.

I like Noilly Prat dry vermouth for quality and value. The general rule of thumb for vermouths is to go French for dry and Italian for sweet. It's wise to store your vermouths, especially your dry vermouths, in the refrigerator, for they will turn and oxidize almost as quickly as a regular bottle of opened wine. This is especially true for dry vermouth; there is enough sugar in sweet vermouth that an opened bottle will last at least a couple weeks. For dry vermouth, I like to save empty 10-ounce club soda bottles. I'll take a big bottle of vermouth and fill the little bottles all the way to the top, then recap them and store them in the refrigerator. This will keep your vermouth fresh. The reason most people think they don't like vermouth is that they've been given bad vermouth at least 90 percent of the time.

I like green olives but don't suggest you put them in this Martini, especially if you're just starting out. Green olives can be fine in a Martini, but it's one of those ingrained, preconceived notions of what a Martini has to be or of people's perception of gin in general. Please look at gin in a fresh light. Automatically putting green olives in a Martini is like always having to wear a tie when a gent puts on a shirt and jacket. Do what you want and feel like.

4 ounces Bombay Sapphire gin   lemon peel spiral

1 ounce cold dry vermouth   green olives, on a 6-inch skewer

1 to 2 dashes orange bitters   (optional)

Into a Boston tin two-thirds full of ice, add the liquid ingredients. Swirl around with a cocktail spoon or a plastic chopstick, whatever you want. Just take your time and make sure you chill it properly. (Use the Force and trust your gut for this step.) Use a Hawthorn strainer and strain contents into a chilled martini glass. Make your lemon spiral over the drink, so the citrus oils mist your cocktail. Serve on a folded linen napkin. Olives are very optional.

	NAME	**Z Is for Zillah**		
	SPIRIT	Gin	GLASS	Martini
	CREATOR	Johnny Michaels		

St-Germain is one of my favorite liqueurs to hit the market in recent years. I used to special-order it out of New York before it was available in Minnesota. After it became distributed here, my contrarian streak kicked in, and I was loath to use it. Now that my head has cooled and logic has returned to the scene, there's no denying what a good product it is. This recipe is very simple, easy, and delicious. I make an illegal bootleg Edward Gorey bev nap for this one. I just recently got turned on to him—he has a very dark style I dig. He has an illustrated alphabet made up of dead children: "Z is for Zillah, who drank too much gin."

Ingredients

4½ ounces Bombay Sapphire gin

½ ounce St-Germain elderflower liqueur

2 lemon wedges or ½ ounce lemon juice (I really prefer Meyer
       lemons, especially in this cocktail)

1 to 2 dashes orange bitters

lemon peel spiral

blood orange wheel, thin (optional)

Into a cobbler shaker 50 percent full of ice, squeeze and add lemon wedges and then add gin, St-Germain, and bitters. Swirl or stir for 13 to 14 seconds and then strain into a chilled martini glass. Garnish with lemon spiral and float blood orange wheel on top (if you wish). The blood orange provides a nice aromatic touch when sipping.

NAME	**The Celestian**
SPIRIT	Gin
GLASS	Martini
CREATOR	Johnny Michaels

Ingredients

3 ounces Tanqueray gin

½ ounce Lime Sour (see p. 189)

½ ounce egg whites (pasteurized egg whites may be substituted but will not produce as good an effect)

½ ounce Green Chartreuse

¼ ounce Luxardo maraschino liqueur

3 dashes peppermint schnapps

2 lime wedges

2 dashes salt solution (see p. 31)

splash cava

2 dashes (approximately ½ ounce) Sour Cherry Sink Syrup (see below)

drizzles Gold and Silver Oils (see below)

brandied cherry, on a 6-inch skewer

key lime wheel

Into an empty Boston tin, squeeze and add lime wedges and then add all the liquid ingredients except cava. Cap and shake vigorously 6 to 7 seconds and then add some ice and shake for another 6 to 7 seconds or so. Strain into martini glass and top with splash of cava. Add Sour Cherry Sink Syrup; it should sink to bottom of glass and ghost, giving drink a nice two-tone fade look. Drizzle cocktail with Gold and Silver Oils and swirl them around with tip of skewer to create a psychedelic effect. Place cherry skewer across top of glass and mount key lime wheel.

Sour Cherry Sink Syrup

I find my sour cherry syrup in Middle Eastern food stores, with brands like Adriatic or Marco Polo. If you can't find it, substitute Monin cherry syrup. You will need to cut the syrup with water, usually fifty-fifty. Used straight out of the bottle, the syrup will sink to the bottom of the glass and refuse to "ghost," or integrate itself into the cocktail.

Ingredients

2 ounces sour cherry syrup

2 ounces water

Store refrigerated in a small bottle, like an empty 10-ounce club soda bottle.

Gold and Silver Oils

Ingredients

2 grams Super Gold Luster Dust

2 grams Nu Silver Luster Dust

4 ounces grapeseed oil, divided

Mix gold dust and 2 ounces of the oil and then, separately, silver dust and the remaining oil. Store each oil in separate 4-ounce eyedropper or miniature squirt bottles. Be sure to shake well daily and also before every use.

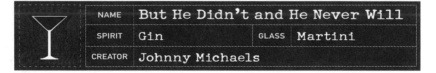

NAME	But He Didn't and He Never Will		
SPIRIT	Gin	GLASS	Martini
CREATOR	Johnny Michaels		

This one gets its name from a Smiths lyric, a running theme in my drink naming. Appropriately, it's a drink of sour grapes (verjus) and bitter tears (salted Fernet-Branca).

Ingredients

3½ ounces New Amsterdam gin
1 ounce White Grape Sour (see p. 191)
½ ounces Fernet-Branca
lemon wedge
2 to 3 dashes (5 to 6 drops) salt solution (see below)
orange peel spiral
3 red grape halves, cut lengthwise, on a 6-inch skewer

Into a Boston tin half full of ice, squeeze and add lemon and then add remaining liquids. Swirl until proper and strain into martini glass. Garnish with orange spiral; place grape skewer across top of glass.

Salt Solution

Ingredients

1 ounce kosher salt
4 ounces hot water

Mix and store in an eyedropper bottle.

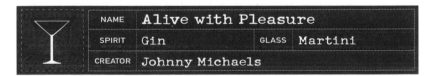

NAME	Alive with Pleasure		
SPIRIT	Gin	GLASS	Martini
CREATOR	Johnny Michaels		

Originally, I made up this drink as a welcome-home present for my friend and business partner Pip Hanson (aka Mr. Pip) when he returned from his one-and-a-half-year foray in Japan. Mr. Pip had decided he was getting out of the bartending business and was moving to Tokyo to utilize his journalism degree by teaching McEnglish. I told him he would be pouring again within a month, and I was right. Mr. Pip had the good fortune of studying under Japan's number-one bartender, Kazuo Uyeda, while he was over there. We exchanged many e-mails discussing bartending philosophies, technique, and bar designs.

This drink was originally called The Return of Mr. Pip. It's a total spring drink—super zesty. Alive with Pleasure has been in my drink-name orphanage for a while, and though I've been waiting to use it on a clear, carbonated cocktail, I think this is a better fit, a good match.

Ingredients

1½ ounces London dry gin

1¼ ounces Yuzu-Ginger Sour (see p. 191)

2 ounces cava (approximately)

½ ounce Cherry Pimm's (see below)

key lime wheel

brandied cherry, on a 6-inch skewer

Add gin and sour to a cobbler shaker around 60 percent full of ice. Shake well and strain into a chilled martini glass until around 70 percent full. Top with cava and give a splash of Cherry Pimm's. The Cherry Pimm's weight will cause it to sink and create a nice two-tone look. Mount key lime wheel on rim of glass and suspend cherry skewer across the top of it.

Cherry Pimm's

Ingredients

4 ounces Pimm's

2 ounces undiluted Adriatic or Marco Polo sour cherry syrup or Monin cherry syrup

Mix Pimm's and syrup and store in an empty 10-ounce club soda or a squirt bottle. Makes enough for 12 cocktails.

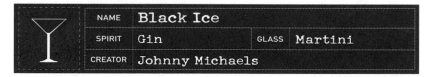

	NAME	Black Ice		
	SPIRIT	Gin	GLASS	Martini
	CREATOR	Johnny Michaels		

This was the first Fernet-Branca cocktail I ever created. It tastes like licking the dirty, frozen pavement at three a.m. in February. Don't ask me how I know, because I can't remember.

Ingredients

3½ ounces No. 9 gin (or any old-school London dry or juniper-
   forward gin)

½ ounce Fernet-Branca

¾ ounce Lemon Sour (see p. 189)

3 dashes peppermint schnapps

2 dashes salt solution (see p. 31)

lemon wedge

lemon peel spiral

Into a Boston tin half full of ice, squeeze and add lemon and then add the liquid ingredients. Swirl plenty until proper and strain into chilled martini glass. Garnish with lemon spiral.

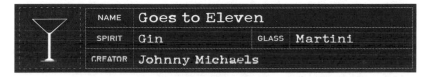

NAME	Goes to Eleven		
SPIRIT	Gin	GLASS	Martini
CREATOR	Johnny Michaels		

For years I have had an irrational disdain for unpickled cucumbers. Some stupid plastic-wrapped cucumber is always getting in the way in our cramped garnish coolers. I have also had it with people reverentially talking about Hendrick's gin and its hint of cucumber, as if the bottle had the power to levitate and pour itself, which would be appreciated. Although it might look nice, it is an ergonomic pain in the ass for every bartender everywhere in the world. The gin is nice but a bit overpriced, in my opinion, so just to screw with Hendrick's, I decided to infuse some good-value gin with cucumber. I use New Amsterdam.

This cocktail is named with a *Spinal Tap* reference. The foil-wrapped baby pickle just kills people who have seen the movie. I was informed that things with vinegar react with aluminum foil, so to avoid any unfortunate incidents (and because wrapping those pickles up every day was a pain), we discontinued that part of the garnish and just went with a key lime wheel mounted on the rim and a couple of thin cucumber slices floating on the cocktail's surface. I really don't think anything bad could come of it. You're not supposed to unwrap and eat the pickle, anyway, but you know how people are. I suggest doing it and telling your guests not to eat the pickle. Also, suspend it over the martini glass, as opposed to submerging it.

3½ ounces Cucumber Gin (see p. 199)

1¼ ounces Lime Sour (see p. 189)

2 dashes peppermint schnapps

2 dashes salt solution (see p. 31)

lime wedge

key lime wheel; or

pickled gherkin, wrapped in foil, on a 6-inch skewer; or

cucumber slices

To a Boston shaker half full of ice, add the liquid ingredients, squeeze and add lime, and shake on medium-soft for around 7 seconds. I don't pound this one, because I don't want a bunch of ice chips in it, but you can always double strain it too. Pour into chilled martini glass. Garnish with key lime wheel, and/or foil-wrapped gherkin, or floating cucumber slices.

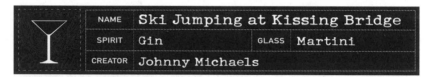

	NAME	Ski Jumping at Kissing Bridge		
	SPIRIT	Gin	GLASS	Martini
	CREATOR	Johnny Michaels		

Kissing Bridge is a ski resort in western New York (I grew up in Buffalo), and ski jumping has always been my favorite Winter Olympics event to watch. This one is about those wonderful early days (and nights) of a budding new romance, when you cross the kissing bridge, as exhilarating as ski jumping, I would imagine. Will you land triumphantly or crash and break your heart?

Ingredients

3½ ounces gin (I like Bombay Sapphire)

½ ounce apple schnapps

3 dashes salt solution (see p. 31)

2 dashes Hot Pepper Tincture (see p. 195)

2 dashes Fee Brothers rhubarb bitters

2 lemon wedges

1 blood orange wheel

1 microflower (I like pansies)

Into a cobbler shaker three-quarters full of ice, squeeze and add lemon wedges and then add the liquid ingredients. Cap and shake on medium 5 to 6 seconds. Strain into martini glass, float blood orange wheel on surface, and place pansy on top of that.

	NAME	Gilbert Perrault		
	SPIRIT	Gin	GLASS	Martini
	CREATOR	Johnny Michaels		

Gilbert Perrault was the star center on the fabled French Connection line for the Buffalo Sabres hockey team in the 1970s, when I was growing up in western New York. I thought about garnishing this one with a few white pieces of Chiclets gum, since most players at the time where missing about half their teeth, but, even though I still think it's funny, decided against it. This to me is a very elegant and wintery gin cocktail. I've described it by saying it's kind of like standing on a sheet of ice, drinking a gin martini, and smoking a menthol cigarette.

Ingredients

3½ ounces Citadelle gin	lemon peel spiral
¾ ounce Yellow Chartreuse	brandied cherry, on a 6-inch
heavy dash peppermint schnapps	skewer
2 to 3 lemon wedges	

Into a Boston tin three-quarters full of ice, squeeze and add lemon wedges and then add the liquid ingredients. Swirl until proper and strain into chilled martini glass. Garnish with lemon spiral and lay skewer across top of glass.

	NAME	City of Light		
	SPIRIT	Gin	GLASS	Martini
	CREATOR	Johnny Michaels		

This was our leadoff specialty cocktail when La Bell Vie opened in Minneapolis. I dug the name (and yeah, I know it's "lights," but I thought "light" sounded better). It had all-French ingredients, and I thought it would be a perfect match for us and

Using a channel knife to make a lemon twist

Spiraling a lemon twist

Two different style twists

would perform well . . . but it did not. It's basically a recalibration of the classic cocktail The White Lady (equal parts gin, Cointreau, and Pernod). I thought that was too sweet, so I turned down the Cointreau and reduced the Pernod to a couple dashes, a teaspoon or so. At that time, the classic cocktail renaissance was already in full swing in New York and other bigger, more cosmopolitan cities. I came to the conclusion that this drink was just like a cool Euro chick with a little too much flavor for Minnesotans at the time, but thankfully things have finally changed over here, helped no doubt by the tireless efforts of bartenders who bend over backward trying to get people to give gin another chance.

Ingredients

4 ounces Citadelle gin

½ ounce Cointreau

3 to 4 good dashes Regan's orange bitters

1 (light) teaspoon Pernod

orange peel spiral

whole star anise

To a Boston tin three-quarters full of ice, add the liquid ingredients and swirl or stir (I'm a swirler) until proper chilling and dilution have been achieved. I use the pinky finger on my swirling hand as a thermometer; it's the only finger that comes in contact with the outside of the tin that's below the waterline. Strain into chilled martini glass, garnish with orange peel, and float star anise.

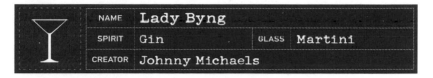

	NAME	Lady Byng		
	SPIRIT	Gin	GLASS	Martini
	CREATOR	Johnny Michaels		

This nice spring-summer martini is named after an NHL award they give out every year to the Most Gentlemanly Player. (Yeah, I don't get it, either.)

Ingredients

3 ounces New Amsterdam gin

½ ounce apricot liqueur

½ ounce vanilla vodka

½ ounce Lemon Sour (see p. 189)

2 to 3 dashes Cardamom Tincture (see p. 196)

2 lemon wedges or ½ ounce lemon juice

orange peel spiral

Into a cobbler shaker three-quarters full of ice, squeeze and add lemon wedges and then add the liquid ingredients. Cap and shake vigorously 5 to 7 seconds. Double strain into martini glass and garnish with orange spiral.

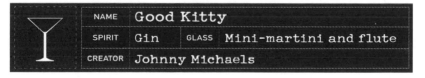

	NAME	Good Kitty		
	SPIRIT	Gin	GLASS	Mini-martini and flute
	CREATOR	Johnny Michaels		

Call me sexist if you want, but I made this one up for the ladies. The fact of the matter is that a lot of them just fawn over the mini–martini glasses we have at La Belle Vie—so cute they rival puppies. This drink is a touch sweet for me. If I was making it to be enjoyed alone, I would add a squeeze of lemon to it, but since it's paired with dry sparkling wine, they complement each other nicely. Champagne or prosecco would work well, too.

1 ounce Bombay Sapphire gin

dash St-Germain elderflower
  liqueur

dash crème de cassis

dash Lemon Sour (see p. 189)

miniature lemon peel spiral

cava (or champagne or prosecco)

To a cobbler shaker half full of ice, add all liquors except sparkling wine. Cap and shake 2 to 3 seconds and then strain into mini–martini glass. Garnish with lemon spiral and fill flute two-thirds full of sparkling wine.

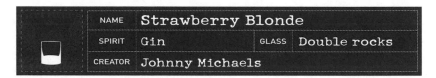

	NAME	Strawberry Blonde		
	SPIRIT	Gin	GLASS	Double rocks
	CREATOR	Johnny Michaels		

This simple summer drink is a great one for converting people to gin. It will turn them out. I use Gordon's or New Amsterdam, depending on whether the customer is intrepid about gin, using the New Amsterdam or Bombay Sapphire for those people.

Ingredients

2 ounces gin

2 ounces Strawberry-Lemon
  Sour (see p. 191)

lemon wheel

strawberry slices

To a pint glass full of ice, add gin and sour. Cap with a Boston tin, shake on medium for 5 seconds, and then pour contents into double rocks glass. Insert lemon wheel and fan strawberry slices on top of surface. For a Strawberry Blonde 2.0, just add a dash or two balsamic vinegar to the gin and sour before shaking.

	NAME	A Sailor Friend		
	SPIRIT	Gin	GLASS	Tall collins
	CREATOR	Johnny Michaels		

This one's named after a Belle and Sebastian lyric. I don't love a ton of sunny, light, upbeat music, but this song and drink both scream spring, to me anyway.

Ingredients

1½ ounces gin

½ ounce Stolichnaya vanilla vodka

1½ ounces Blueberry-Lemon Sour (see p. 191)

2 to 3 dashes Cardamom Tincture (see p. 196)

cold club soda

lemon wheel

6 to 10 fresh blueberries

To a tall collins glass with ice, add all liquids except club soda. Mix with a straw and top off with club soda. Add blueberries, remix, then insert lemon wheel.

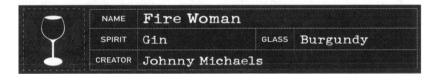

	NAME	Fire Woman		
	SPIRIT	Gin	GLASS	Burgundy
	CREATOR	Johnny Michaels		

I first thought of using wineglasses for feminine martini-style drinks when I did a cocktail list for a raucous party bar of debauchery, where people would be packed in like sardines. One could get jostled around plenty getting from one end of the place to the other without spilling a drop.

Ingredients

1½ ounces gin

1½ ounces Fire Woman Mix (see below)

2 ounces cava

2 blood orange slices

To a pint glass full of ice, add gin and Fire Woman Mix. Cap and give 2 to 3 soft back-and-forth shakes to combine. Pour contents into burgundy wineglass, being careful to hit the bottom part of the glass, where the bowl meets the stem and the glass is the strongest. Top with cava and give a quick stir with a plastic chopstick, thin-bladed knife, or spoon. Float blood orange slices on the drink's surface.

Fire Woman Mix

Ingredients

10 ounces pulp-free orange juice concentrate, defrosted
10 ounces Monin blood orange syrup
1 teaspoon orange bitters.

Mix, store in a bottle, and refrigerate. Makes enough for about 7 cocktails.

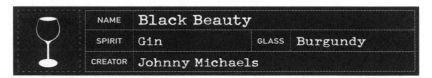

NAME	Black Beauty		
SPIRIT	Gin	GLASS	Burgundy
CREATOR	Johnny Michaels		

I almost always have a punch-style drink, designed for the ladies and served in a big burgundy wineglass, on our little list. I look at our little list as our starting lineup and the expanded drink list as our bench players. I use seasonal and perishable fruit mixes only on the little list because they wouldn't sell fast enough on the big list and we'd lose money. I also like to be vague in my menu descriptions or flavor profiles so people don't know there's gin in it unless they ask. Sometimes they order it, dig it, ask, and then are shocked. I almost always make a premix for my punches so that we just have to use one bottle when we're busy, instead of four.

Ingredients

2 ounces gin
½ ounce St-Germain elderflower
    liqueur
¼ ounce crème de cassis
¼ ounce Monin lavender syrup
dash orange bitters

2 to 3 drops orange flower water
2 ounces cava (approximately)
orange slice
1 lychee fruit (canned)
1 fresh raspberry

To a pint glass full of ice, add all the liquid ingredients except cava. Cap with a Boston tin and give it 2 to 3 shakes. Pour contents into burgundy glass (be careful and try to hit the bottom part of the glass, where the bowl meets the stem and the glass is the strongest). Top with cava and give a quick stir. Garnish drink's surface with fruit.

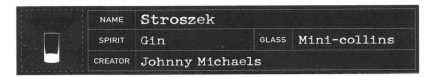

NAME	Stroszek		
SPIRIT	Gin	GLASS	Mini-collins
CREATOR	Johnny Michaels		

I describe this one as top-shelf ice fishing liquor. If you've ever seen Werner Herzog's film *Stroszek*, you'll know what I mean when I say it captures the feeling of a frozen and harsh midwestern winter very well. That's why I guess this drink makes me think of ice fishing, the taste of a cold and lonely winter.

At La Belle Vie I premix the stuff and refrigerate it. It gets shaken slightly with the ice it's served with, but less dilution occurs because the liquor is cold and it's only lightly shaken. If you try this drink and like it, maybe you'll want to commit to premixing a bottle and leaving it in the refrigerator. It doesn't go bad. This recipe is a home version.

Ingredients

2 ounces Beefeater gin

½ ounce Luxardo maraschino liqueur

2 dashes Caraway Tincture (see p. 195)

2 dashes peppermint schnapps

2 dashes Fee Brothers old-fashioned bitters

brandied cherry, on a 5-inch skewer

Combine all the liquid ingredients in a Boston tin and place in freezer. After 15 minutes, remove from freezer and add a few ice cubes. Cap with a pint glass and shake briefly and gently and then pour contents into mini-collins glass. Garnish with brandied cherry.

NAME	Rano Pano		
SPIRIT	Gin	GLASS	Double rocks
CREATOR	Johnny Michaels		

This one makes a great summer punch party cocktail. It's named after a Mogwai song that was my favorite off their new (at the time) record. Drink lists can be like records. If you are fortunate, there are a few on there that make you proud, make you feel lucky to say you thought them up. I'd noticed a lot of the Japanese beverages in Asian food stores had vinegar in them. I'd also noticed people paying four dollars a bottle for Kombuchasomethingorother, which tastes like a fruit drink with a hint of vinegar to me. I'd used balsamic vinegar in cocktails before, so why hadn't I thought of this earlier? Better late than never.

I suggest freezing your watermelon juice immediately after juicing because making the Watermelon Rind Brine will take a few days. Defrost the juice for the Watermelon Pickle Pop when you're ready to make the drink. At the restaurant we have pitchers of the cocktail premixed, so when you get a drink ticket, it's as easy as filling a glass with ice, pouring in the finished cocktail, and garnishing with a lemon wheel. FastFastFast! The rind brine and gin help keep the watermelon juice fresh, but it still only has a shelf life of a couple days.

Ingredients

2 parts gin
3 parts Pickled Watermelon Sour (see below)
lemon wheel

In a pitcher with a cover, mix liquids at a ratio of 2 parts gin to 3 parts Pickled Watermelon Sour. Will keep refrigerated 2 days. To serve, pour cocktail into a double rocks glass filled with ice, stir, and garnish with lemon wheel.

Pickled Watermelon Sour

Ingredients

16 ounces watermelon juice, defrosted
8 ounces Watermelon Rind Brine (see below)
12 ounces Lemon Sour (see p. 189)
1 ounce white vinegar
1 ounce salt solution (see p. 31)

Mix all ingredients in a pitcher, and cover and refrigerate.

Watermelon Rind Brine

Ingredients

$\frac{1}{3}$ to $\frac{1}{2}$ of a watermelon's rind   1 cup sugar

1 cup water   1 cup white wine vinegar

Juice watermelon and then freeze juice to keep it fresh while making brine. Cut white part of rind away from green shell and discard shell. It's a bit easier to shave off the outside green rind with a Y-shaped vegetable peeler and not so easy with the stick-shaped peelers. Cut white rind into small, compactable pieces. In a small pot, heat water, sugar, and white wine vinegar until sugar dissolves. Place rind pieces in a mason jar or any sealable container. Glass is preferred because it doesn't absorb the flavor the way plastics sometimes will. Pour in brine, making sure all pieces are covered. Seal jar or container and place in refrigerator for at least 3 to 4 days. Strain out rind pieces, and refrigerate brine.

NAME	No Future		
SPIRIT	Gin	GLASS	Rocks
CREATOR	Johnny Michaels		

I describe this drink as a summer gin old-fashioned. In the summer of 2010, I was privileged to be asked to help judge the Twin Cities' leg of Bombay Sapphire's 2010 Most Inspired Bartender contest, the only true cocktail contest for us in these parts at the time. We Twin Cites bartenders all appreciate Bombay Sapphire for the exceptional job they do with the event every year. (I was lucky enough to win in 2008, a cherished memory.) It was an honor and a privilege hanging out with then–Bombay Sapphire brand ambassador Milo Rodriguez, an Oxford-educated man who bartended at Milk and Honey in London for a couple years. We're talking Real Deal Holyfield! That was the highlight of my summer, picking his brain and listening to what the current cocktail culture was like in different cities and countries.

A lot of these Bombay Sapphire contest cocktails have names with "queen" in their titles, which got me thinking of "God Save the Queen," by The Sex Pistols. A prominent lyric in that song is "no future," which for some unknown reason appealed to me. I got a kick out of it all summer when drink tickets would pop up and "No Future" would be staring me in the face.

Ingredients

2 ounces Bombay Sapphire gin
½ ounce Yellow Chartreuse
dash peppermint schnapps
dash salt solution (see p. 31)
2 lemon wheels
orange wheel
brandied cherry or green olive, on a 6-inch skewer

To a rocks glass, add lemon and orange wheels (I like sandwiching the orange wheel), Yellow Chartreuse (which we are using instead of sugar or simple syrup, adding complexity and synergizing with the gin), peppermint schnapps, and salt solution. Using a flat-bottomed wooden muddler, crush the citrus fruit, trying to release the oils from the peel and juice the fruit without pulverizing everything. Flat crush the fruit with slow-power muddles—no jackhammering or pounding required. As Jack Nicolson says in *Chinatown*, "Some things in life take a bit of finesse." Add the gin and swirl the glass so that everything mixes together. Top off with ice and insert skewered cherry or olive.

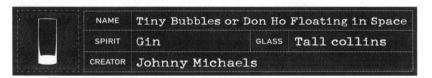

	NAME	Tiny Bubbles or Don Ho Floating in Space		
	SPIRIT	Gin	GLASS	Tall collins
	CREATOR	Johnny Michaels		

This is my version of a cruise ship drink. I like to put it on the menu in January and February, when people need a vacation in a glass. I've installed it at several places and under both names. I personally love the thought of Don Ho Floating in Space but felt Tiny Bubbles was a better fit for La Belle Vie. This drink refuses to stop selling. I'm constantly surprised by how many sophisticated diners love this drink. I am a bit embarrassed to admit how simple and easy this one is to make, but it's ridiculously cost effective and puts points on my team's board. I am prepared to be lashed by the insults of serious and proper mixologists everywhere, but at the end of the day, I work at a fine-dining restaurant, and we would like to keep the doors open. So if this is what makes people happy and us money, I will do it.

Ingredients

1 ounce London dry gin	1½ ounces cava (approximately)
½ ounce Cruzan pineapple rum	orange wheel
⅛ ounce Soho lychee liqueur	1 lychee fruit (canned)
1½ ounces guava juice (approximately)	red maraschino cherry (I know, I know)

To a tall collins glass with ice, add gin, rum, and lychee liqueur. Add a few more cubes to glass, add guava juice, and mix with a straw. Top with cava and give the drink a poke or two with straw to finish mixing. Insert orange wheel, lychee fruit, and cherry onto drink's surface.

NAME	My Paranormal Romance		
SPIRIT	Gin	GLASS	Burgundy
CREATOR	Johnny Michaels		

This drink was inspired while snacking on our secret stash of candy. We have little cups of the stuff that we keep behind the bar to help us rock out our eight- to twelve-hour aerobic bartending sessions. One day I was eating a combo of Jolly Joes and extra-hot Hot Tamales, and the light bulb turned on. This drink has evolved and had several names. A drink often keeps getting updated and improved and might take a year or two until it stops growing. This one is now done because, basically, I have maxed out the equalizer on all the flavors. I try to involve the whole tongue in this one: sweet, salty, spicy, tangy, bitter. Not much bitter, though. This one is zesty, a mix of crazy, explosive flavors. It's not for everybody, but I like those kinds of things, in drinks, movies, people. I wrap three blaze-orange rubber bands around the glass, which contrast nicely with the purple color of the drink—one of my beginning attempts at creating psychedelic cocktails.

Ingredients

1½ ounces London dry gin

1½ ounces My Paranormal Romance Mix (see below); or

    ¾ ounce Concord grape juice concentrate, defrosted

¾ ounce Lemon Sour (see p. 189)

heavy dash absinthe

dash salt solution (see p. 31)

dash peppermint schnapps

dash Cinnamon Tincture (see p. 196)

dash Hot Pepper Tincture (see p. 195)

2 ounces cava (approximately)

orange slice

apple slice, on a 6-inch skewer

To a pint glass full of ice, add gin and either the My Paranormal Romance Mix or the on-the-fly version of the mix included in the ingredient list. Cap and shake 3 to 4 times. Pour contents into burgundy wineglass (with three blaze-orange rubber bands wrapped around it), being careful to have mixture hit the bottom of glass upon entry, not the thin, fragile sides. Top with cava and gently stir with a plastic chopstick. Float orange slice on the drink's surface and then insert skewered apple slice so that it dangles over the surface, which looks cool.

My Paranormal Romance Mix

Ingredients

10 ounces Concord grape juice concentrate, defrosted

10 ounces Lemon Sour (see p. 189)

1 ounce absinthe (I use Vieux Carré)

½ ounce salt solution (see p. 31)

¼ ounce Hot Pepper Tincture (see p. 195)

½ ounce balsamic vinegar

¼ ounce Cinnamon Tincture (see p. 196)

¼ ounce peppermint schnapps

Mix all ingredients and store in a 24-ounce squirt bottle. Makes enough for 16 cocktails, so have a party.

NAME	Planet Junípero and Moon		
SPIRIT	Gin	GLASS	White wine and mini-collins
CREATOR	Johnny Michaels		

This drink was supposed to be the center of a much more overblown drink that I waited until the last minute to try out, and it just didn't work. So now it is Planet and Moon, a sci-fi version of a bump and a beer. I'm really into the idea of separating things, sipping back and forth.

Ingredients

2 ounces Junípero gin

2 ounces cold club soda

½ ounce Moon Mix (see below)

Pour gin into white wine glass and add some ice, enough to chill and slightly dilute gin without washing it out completely, like 2 or 3 chips or a cube or two. Pour club soda into mini-collins glass filled with ice, add Moon Mix, and stir with black stir/sipper straw.

Moon Mix

Ingredients

4 ounces raw honey

4 ounces lemon juice

½ ounce white balsamic vinegar

Stir all ingredients until honey is dissolved, and store in an air-tight bottle.

NAME	This Charming Man		
SPIRIT	Gin	GLASS	Double rocks
CREATOR	Johnny Michaels		

Here's another of my many drinks named after a Smiths song or lyric. Mr. Pip once had an idea for a cocktail that would come with a pile of tobacco and a rolling paper. I didn't like that idea so much, but it triggered me into getting this one. We garnish this drink with an all-white Dunhill International Lights cigarette, served on the side in a tall, skinny shot glass with some strike-anywhere matches. Even nonsmokers like this. They like to touch and play with the cigarette, for they'd never ask a smoking friend for one and waste it with prices being what they are nowadays.

Ingredients

1½ ounces Bombay Sapphire gin
½ ounce Lemon Sour (see p. 189)
¼ ounce crème de cassis
2 ounces cava (approximately)
lemon wheel
cigarette sidecar with strike-anywhere matches

To a double rocks glass with ice, add gin, sour, and crème de cassis. Mix with a stir straw and then top with cava, gently poking and restirring to blend, protecting the carbonation. Insert lemon wheel into drink and serve with cigarette sidecar.

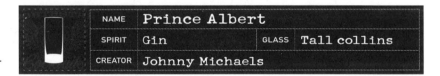

NAME	Prince Albert		
SPIRIT	Gin	GLASS	Tall collins
CREATOR	Johnny Michaels		

This is a great, refreshing summer cocktail—something different for the default gin and tonic lover to try. I'll be making this one until I kick the bucket. I won the 2008 Bombay Sapphire contest in the Twin Cities with this one and got my picture in GQ for it (as if the Mayan calendar's ending wasn't enough to worry about).

The key flavor in Earl Grey tea is bergamot oil, which is tart. My fresh lemon sour is balanced the way I want it for making a whatever sour or a lemonade. I've included the additional simple syrup to account for the added tartness of the bergamot oil. Adjust for personal taste. If one substituted defrosted lemonade concentrate for the lemon sour, the simple syrup could probably be skipped. The extra ice cubes are added to account for the melting that occurs when adding room-temperature gin. If I didn't do this, I'd end up adding a higher percentage of club soda to the drink, resulting in a slightly watery cocktail—and I try to make perfect cocktails. To make an extra-bracing and refreshing drink, store the gin in the freezer before using, a great trick for any soda or tonic drink served on hot, sunny days.

Ingredients

2 ounces Earl Grey Gin (see p. 198)   cold club soda or plain seltzer
1 ounce Lemon Sour (see p. 189)   lemon wheel
¼ ounce simple syrup (see p. 181)   6-inch skewer

To a tall collins glass with ice, add gin, sour, and simple syrup. Stir with a straw, add a few more ice cubes, and then top with club soda. Take 6-inch skewer and break off 2 inches. With your now 4-inch skewer, pierce lemon wheel where the pith meets the rind and place skewer over glass so that most of lemon wheel is submerged in cocktail.

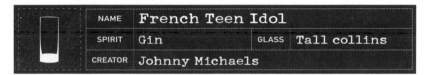

NAME	French Teen Idol		
SPIRIT	Gin	GLASS	Tall collins
CREATOR	Johnny Michaels		

This one I named after a Spanish one-man electronic instrumental artist. It has several French ingredients and is not served with ice. I also read once (yeah, once) that French teenagers liked to drink Pernod, Grenadine, and soda in tall collins glasses. I collect these random puzzle pieces. They clutter what's left of my brain (what a mess). But every now and then, they just come together. I don't know how it happens, but I can tell you I don't take credit for it. Sometimes, you can just tell there are forces at work, and I ask no questions. Like the logic-defying, enormous, perfectly fitting stone blocks of the pyramids. Somebody helped, and they didn't sign their name on it.

Ingredients

1 ounce Citadelle gin   ¾ ounce Lemon Sour (see p. 189)
¾ ounce Green Chartreuse   ½ ounce fresh lemon juice
¾ ounce absinthe   1 lemon wedge
¾ ounce Adriatic or Marco Polo   cold club soda
    sour cherry syrup or Monin   lemon wheel
    cherry syrup

To a Boston shaker half full of ice, squeeze and add lemon wedge and all liquid ingredients except club soda and powershake 5 to 6 seconds. Strain into empty tall collins glass until one-quarter full. Top with cold club soda until the glass is half full (I mean empty). Garnish by placing the lemon wheel flat on drink's surface.

NAME	I'm Your Huckleberry		
SPIRIT	Gin	GLASS	Rocks
CREATOR	Megan Arts		

Ingredients

2½ ounces Tanqueray gin

1½ ounces Moritz Thienelt blackberry liqueur

1 (heavy) ounce fresh lime juice

¾ ounce Monin huckleberry syrup

2 blueberries, on a skewer

Shake with ice and strain into ice-filled rocks glass. Garnish with skewered blueberries.

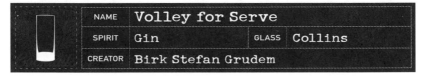

NAME	Mirror of Venus		
SPIRIT	Gin	GLASS	Coupe with sidecar
CREATOR	Jourdan Gomez		

Ingredients

2 ounces Bols Genever

¾ ounce fresh lemon juice

¾ ounce Monin jasmine syrup

1 egg white

¾ (light) ounce heavy cream

3 drops orange flower water

Rothman & Winter crème de violette

Rinse coupe with crème de violette, discarding excess. Shake remaining ingredients without ice. Add ice and shake again. Strain and serve.

NAME	Volley for Serve		
SPIRIT	Gin	GLASS	Collins
CREATOR	Birk Stefan Grudem		

Ingredients

1 ounce Chamomile Gin (see p. 200)

1 ounce Pimm's

½ ounce Yellow Chartreuse

½ ounce fresh lemon juice

1 ounce fresh honeydew melon juice

13 drops Bittercube Bolivar bitters

cold club soda

3 mint sprigs

Shake all the liquid ingredients with ice and strain into ice-filled collins glass. Top with soda and bitters. Garnish with mint sprigs.

	NAME	Oliveto		
	SPIRIT	Gin	GLASS	Rocks
	CREATOR	Pip Hanson		

Make the salt solution at a ratio of 1 part kosher salt to 3 parts hot water and the simple syrup at a ratio of 2 parts sugar to 1 part water.

Ingredients

2 (heavy) ounces Martin Miller Westbourne gin

1 teaspoon Licor 43

½ ounce simple syrup

1 ounce lemon juice

½ ounce olive oil

egg white

dash salt solution

Preshake all ingredients without ice, add ice, and then shake again. Strain into rocks glass.

	NAME	The Secret Life		
	SPIRIT	Gin	GLASS	Champagne
	CREATOR	Pip Hanson		

Make the honey syrup by dissolving 2 parts honey in 1 part boiling water. Make the salt solution at a ratio of 1 part kosher salt to 3 parts hot water.

Ingredients

1½ (light) ounces Tanqueray gin

1 ounce honey syrup

½ ounce fresh lemon juice

dash (about 12 drops) salt solution

2 ounces Gruet or other sparkling wine (approximately)

Shake all ingredients, except sparkling wine, with ice and strain into champagne flute. Top with wine.

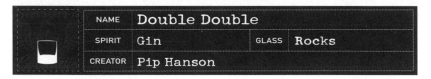

	NAME	Double Double		
	SPIRIT	Gin	GLASS	Rocks
	CREATOR	Pip Hanson		

Ingredients

1½ ounces Beefeater gin

¾ ounce Campari

½ ounce Carpano Antica sweet vermouth

½ ounce Punt e Mes vermouth

¼ ounce Cynar

orange peel coin

Stir all the liquid ingredients in a mixing glass with ice and strain into chilled rocks glass. Squeeze orange coin over drink to express oils and drop in.

	NAME	Mr. Bitterness		
	SPIRIT	Gin	GLASS	Sour
	CREATOR	Pip Hanson		

Ingredients

1 ounce Tanqueray gin

1 (heavy) ounce grapefruit juice

1 (heavy) ounce Campari

¾ ounce Green Chartreuse

1 ounce cold club soda (approximately)

lime wheel, skewered on opposite sides so that the lime wheel

hangs like a *U*

Shake all the liquid ingredients, except soda, with ice and strain into sour glass. Top with soda and lay lime wheel skewer across the top of glass, face down in defeat.

	NAME	**Fireflower**		
	SPIRIT	Gin	GLASS	Collins
	CREATOR	Pip Hanson		

Ingredients

dash Tabasco

dash orange bitters

3 drops orange flower water

¼ ounce St-Germain elderflower liqueur

2 ounces Plymouth gin

orange juice

red pepper flakes

In a collins glass filled with ice, build in order given and top with orange juice. Garnish with red pepper flakes sprinkled on the surface.

	NAME	**Blueberry Boat**		
	SPIRIT	Gin	GLASS	Champagne
	CREATOR	Pip Hanson		

Make the simple syrup at a ratio of 2 parts sugar to 1 part water.

Ingredients

3 ounces Tanqueray gin

12 blueberries

5 basil leaves

1 ounce fresh lemon juice

¾ ounce simple syrup

Muddle basil and blueberries in the bottom of a shaker. Add ice and remaining ingredients and shake. Strain with a Hawthorn strainer and a fine-mesh strainer into chilled champagne flute. Garnish with a few blueberries.

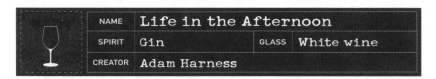

NAME	Life in the Afternoon		
SPIRIT	Gin	GLASS	White wine
CREATOR	Adam Harness		

This is a simple riff on a French 75. The name has nothing to do with Hemmingway's Death in the Afternoon cocktail. I came up with this drink to get people out of the box with their vodka habits. The gin is softened with the round cucumber and chamomile flavors.

Ingredients

2 ounces London dry gin
1 ounce Cucumber-Mint-
    Chamomile Syrup (see p. 185)

¼ lemon, squeezed
cava
long lemon twist

Shake gin, syrup, and lemon juice with ice. Strain into white wine glass and top with cava. Garnish with lemon twist.

NAME	Black Gimlet		
SPIRIT	Gin	GLASS	Coupe
CREATOR	Adam Harness		

Riffing ain't easy, but it's necessary. I love the sharp citrus and pepper notes in Right gin. It takes to black peppercorns better than any gin I've used.

Ingredients

2½ ounces Black Pepper Right Gin (see p. 201)
½ ounce Lime Sour (see p. 189)
freshly cracked black pepper

Shake gin and sour violently with ice. Strain with a Hawthorn strainer and a fine-mesh strainer into coupe. Garnish with black pepper.

NAME	Violet Crush		
SPIRIT	Gin	GLASS	Collins
CREATOR	Adam Harness		

Ingredients

2 ounces London dry gin
¾ ounce mangosteen juice
½ ounce crème de violette

¼ lemon, squeezed
club soda
lemon twist

Shake all the liquid ingredients except club soda and strain into collins glass over rocks. Top with soda and garnish with lemon twist.

NAME	Going Dutch		
SPIRIT	Gin	GLASS	Rocks
CREATOR	Jesse Held		

Ingredients

1½ ounces Bols Genever
½ (heavy) ounce maraschino
 liqueur
½ ounce Dolin blanc vermouth

¼ ounce fresh lemon juice
lemon twist
thyme sprig, lightly rubbed

Shake the liquid ingredients with ice and strain into ice-filled rocks glass. Garnish with thyme and lemon twist.

NAME	Swiss Guard		
SPIRIT	Gin	GLASS	Coupe
CREATOR	Rob Jones		

Ingredients

2 ounces Farmer's gin
¾ ounce Rothman & Winter apricot liqueur

¾ ounce Cocchi Aperitivo Americano
¾ ounce fresh lemon juice
Kubler absinthe

Rinse coupe with absinthe, discarding excess. Shake remaining liquid ingredients
with ice and strain into coupe.

	NAME	Algernon's Afterparty		
	SPIRIT	Gin	GLASS	Coupe
	CREATOR	Rob Jones		

Ingredients

1¾ ounces Death's Door gin
½ ounce St-Germain elderflower
   liqueur
¼ ounce absinthe

¼ ounce Senior orange curaçao
3 drops orange flower water
½ ounce fresh lemon juice
¾ ounce fresh grapefruit juice

Shake all ingredients with ice and strain into coupe.

	NAME	Manic Myrtil		
	SPIRIT	Gin	GLASS	Martini
	CREATOR	Shawn Jones		

Ingredients

2 ounces New Amsterdam gin
1 ounce St-Germain elderflower liqueur
Juice from ½ lemon
½ ounce Monin blueberry syrup
2 dashes Tabasco
2 basil leaves, slapped

Shake all ingredients with ice and strain into martini glass. Garnish with fresh
basil leaf.

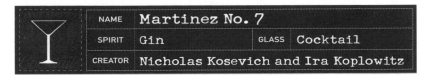

NAME	Martinez No. 7		
SPIRIT	Gin	GLASS	Cocktail
CREATOR	Nicholas Kosevich and Ira Koplowitz		

Ingredients

2 ounces Plymouth gin

½ ounce Carpano Antica sweet vermouth

½ ounce Noilly Prat dry vermouth

¼ ounce Luxardo maraschino liqueur

15 drops Bittercube orange bitters

2 cucumber slices

pinch salt

Lightly muddle one of the cucumber slices and salt in a mixing glass. Add the liquid ingredients, stir, and strain into cocktail glass. Garnish with the remaining cucumber slice.

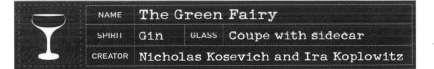

NAME	The Green Fairy		
SPIRIT	Gin	GLASS	Coupe with sidecar
CREATOR	Nicholas Kosevich and Ira Koplowitz		

Ingredients

2 ounces Bombay Sapphire gin

¾ ounce Green Tea Syrup (see p. 187)

¾ ounce fresh lemon juice

1 egg white

7 drops St. George absinthe

Shake all ingredients, except absinthe, without ice. Shake again with ice and strain into coupe and sidecar. Top with absinthe.

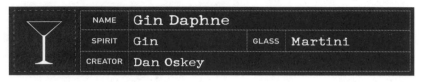

NAME	Gin Daphne		
SPIRIT	Gin	GLASS	Martini
CREATOR	Dan Oskey		

Ingredients

2 ounces Hendrick's gin
½ ounce St-Germain elderflower liqueur
juice from ¼ lime
½ ounce lemonade
spicy ginger beer (Gosling's)
lime wedge

Shake liquid ingredients, except ginger beer, with ice and strain into martini glass. Top with ginger beer and garnish with lime wedge.

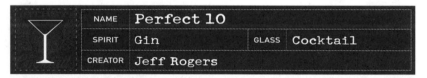

NAME	Perfect 10		
SPIRIT	Gin	GLASS	Cocktail
CREATOR	Jeff Rogers		

Ingredients

2 ounces Bombay Sapphire gin
¾ ounce Tuaca liqueur
¾ ounce Fanatical Botanical Syrup (see p. 188)
candied lemon peel
black licorice piece

Combine liquid ingredients in a mixing glass two-thirds full of ice. Stir until chilled and strain into chilled cocktail glass. Garnish with candied lemon peel and licorice.

NAME	JRO's Gin Fizz	
SPIRIT	Gin	GLASS Champagne
CREATOR	Jeff Rogers	

Ingredients

1 ounce London dry gin

½ ounce fresh orange juice

¼ ounce fresh lime juice

¼ ounce Clove Syrup (see p. 189)

¼ ounce St. Elizabeth Allspice Dram

2 drops orange flower water

½ ounce half-and-half

1 pasteurized egg white

cold club soda

large orange twist, plugged with 3 cloves

In a Boston shaker, shake vigorously all liquid ingredients, except club soda, without ice 10 to 15 seconds. Fill shaker two-thirds with cracked ice and shake vigorously until a light frost appears on the outside of shaker or your arms fall off, whichever comes first. Strain into chilled champagne flute and top with club soda. Garnish with orange twist and enjoy.

NAME	Emerald Buddha	
SPIRIT	Gin	GLASS Rocks
CREATOR	Sonya Runkle and Geoffrey Trelstad	

This is a subtly energizing summer patio sipper.

Ingredients

2 ounces Beefeater gin

1½ ounces Agwa de Bolivia coca leaf liqueur

fresh grapefruit juice

5 drops Fee Brothers peach bitters

2 lemon wedges

2 lime wedges

Squeeze one of the lemon and one of the lime wedges into rocks glass. Add gin, liqueur, and bitters and stir. Fill glass with ice and top with splash of grapefruit juice. Garnish with remaining lemon and lime wedges and a sipping straw.

Ingredients

2 ounces Bombay Sapphire gin

½ ounce Sato no Homare sake

¾ ounce Cherry-Yuzu Base (see below)

lemon wedge

½ yuzu powder, ½ sugar mixture

1 bing cherry, halved

1 Toasted Thai Chili Marshmallow (see below)

Rub half the rim of a chilled martini glass with lemon wedge and coat with yuzu-sugar mixture. Shake the liquid ingredients vigorously with ice and strain into glass. Garnish with cherry halves and marshmallow skewered on a chopstick.

Cherry-Yuzu Base

Ingredients

2 cups sour cherry purée

1¾ cups sugar

⅓ cup yuzu juice

Heat cherry purée and sugar until sugar dissolves. Let cool, incorporate yuzu juice, and refrigerate.

Toasted Thai Chili Marshmallows

Ingredients

2 to 3 Thai chilies, chopped

¼ cup corn syrup

1⅓ cups egg whites (about 9½ large eggs)

10 sheets gelatin, soaked per manufacturer's instructions

cornstarch, for dusting marshmallows

2 tablespoons water

2 cups sugar

Heat chilies with corn syrup and water until mixture starts to boil and immediately remove from heat. Pass mixture through a fine sieve, making sure to press chilies against side. Add sugar and a little more water to create a wet-sand texture. In a separate bowl, whip egg whites on low speed to create soft peaks. Using a candy thermometer, cook sugar mixture to 311°F and add soaked gelatin. Pour gelatin-sugar mixture into egg whites. Whip mixture until cool and pour onto a half sheet pan lined with plastic wrap. Dust top of marshmallow block with cornstarch, flip, remove plastic wrap, and dust the other side. Let sit 5 to 6 hours and then cut into small cubes. Makes approximately 2 dozen marshmallows.

	NAME	Sweet Debacle		
	SPIRIT	Gin	GLASS	Highball
	CREATOR	Thea Sheffert		

Ingredients

2 ounces Bombay Sapphire gin

1 nectarine quarter

2 to 3 basil leaves

¾ ounce Brown Sugar Syrup
(see p. 182)

lemon wedge

splash club soda

small scoop Nectarine-
Champagne Sorbet
(see below)

Muddle nectarine, basil, and lemon wedge in a pint glass. Fill glass with ice and add gin and syrup. Cap and shake and then strain through a Hawthorn strainer and a fine-mesh strainer into ice-filled highball. Top with club soda and sorbet.

Nectarine-Champagne Sorbet

Ingredients

⅔ cup sugar

1 cup water

2½ pounds ripe nectarines, peeled, halved, and pitted

½ teaspoon fresh lemon zest

3 tablespoons fresh lemon juice

¾ cup champagne

Bring sugar and water to a boil in a large saucepan over medium-high heat and boil mixture 4 minutes. Add nectarines and cook over medium heat, stirring frequently, 5 minutes for ripe fruit or 3 minutes for overly ripe fruit. Remove mixture from heat, stir in lemon zest and juice and, and let cool at room temperature 5 to 10 minutes. Purée mixture until smooth in a food processor or with an immersion blender. Allow purée to cool, mix in champagne, and then freeze in an ice cream maker according to the manufacturer's instructions. Makes enough for 6 to 8 cocktails.

NAME	Sake It Me Pera		
SPIRIT	Gin	GLASS	Martini
CREATOR	Thea Sheffert		

This drink includes Velvet Falernum, a rum-based lime, almond, and clove liqueur.

Ingredients

2½ ounces Bombay Sapphire gin

1½ ounces Velvet Falernum

½ ounce Sato no Homare sake

1 comice pear half, cored and seeded

9 to 10 sage leaves

lemon wedge

½ sugar, ½ freshly ground nutmeg mixture

lemon peel coin

pear slice

Rub half the rim of a martini glass with lemon wedge and coat with nutmeg-sugar mixture. In a shaker, muddle pear half and 7 to 8 of the sage leaves. Add ice and the liquid ingredients and shake. Strain with a Hawthorn strainer and a fine-mesh strainer into martini glass. Squeeze lemon coin over top and discard. Garnish with pear slice and remaining sage leaves.

NAME	Summer Queen		
SPIRIT	Gin	GLASS	Martini
CREATOR	Andy Truskolaski		

Ingredients

2 ounces Bombay Sapphire gin

1 ounce pineapple juice

½ ounce simple syrup (see p. 181)

½ ounce fresh lime juice

½ ounce Licor 43

3 dashes green Tabasco

1 egg white

3 sage leaves

lime wedge

Orange-infused Rock Salt (see below)

Rub half the rim of a martini glass with lime wedge and coat with rock salt. Tear up sage leaves and place in a mixing glass and then add Tabasco. Add ice and remaining ingredients and shake vigorously. Strain into martini glass.

Orange-infused Rock Salt

Ingredients

½ cup sugar

½ cup rock salt

4 ounces orange zest

Place all ingredients in a food processor and blend until fine.

Vodka

NAME	Parlez-Vous		
SPIRIT	Vodka	GLASS	Martini
CREATOR	Johnny Michaels		

When we first opened La Belle Vie in 2005, I thought the City of Light, which was all French ingredients and gin based, would be our signature cocktail, but people just weren't hitting on gin around here six years ago like they are now (better late than never!). This drink idea came to me all at once, maybe within ten seconds, the entire drink and its name, which is unusual. I normally cobble these cocktails together, sometimes waiting months for the missing piece of the puzzle to appear. This cocktail has been batting leadoff ever since it was put on the list, and it might never leave that spot. It's a real favorite with the ladies.

Ingredients

1 ounce raspberry vodka

1 ounce pineapple juice

¼ ounce Chambord raspberry liqueur

2½ ounces cava

Parlez-Vous Foam (see below)

orange peel spiral

raspberry, on a 6-inch skewer

To a cobbler shaker half full of ice, add vodka and pineapple juice, swirl for a bit, and then let still chill. Meanwhile, fill a double rocks glass half full of foam and set aside. Pour contents of shaker into chilled martini glass and top with cava, leaving around one-quarter of the glass's depth for foam. Drizzle in Chambord to create a shaded two-tone effect. Stir foam with a spoon, making it more pourable, and then top cocktail with foam. Garnish with orange spiral and skewered raspberry.

Parlez-Vous Foam

Ingredients

9 sheets platinum-grade leaf gelatin
2 cups pulp-free tangerine-orange juice
2 cups simple syrup (see p. 181)
4 cups Boiron passion fruit purée, defrosted in refrigerator
   overnight

Bloom gelatin in tangerine-orange juice and simple syrup until soft, at least 15 minutes. Heat mixture in a saucepan, whisking constantly. Remove from heat as soon as gelatin melts (the liquid will have a thin layer of foam). Combine and whisk mixture and passion fruit purée. Refrigerate mixture: it will become gelatinous. Using a pastry bag, fill a whipped cream dispenser three-quarters full with mixture, attach top of dispenser, and add nitrous oxide (1 cartridge for a small dispenser and 2 for a large). Shake well and long to combine mixture and gas. Keep canister refrigerated. This recipe fills a large dispenser twice and a small one four times.

Dispensing Parlez-Vous Foam

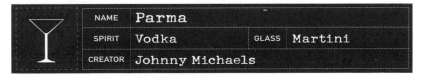

NAME	When in Rome		
SPIRIT	Vodka	GLASS	Martini
CREATOR	Johnny Michaels		

This cocktail is the first Mr. Pip got on the drink list at La Belle Vie. Mr. Pip and I go way back. He started out his career at the Dakota Jazz Club barbacking for me on Saturday nights. We've known each other, worked together, bounced ideas back and forth, laughed and argued for over ten years. We also co-own the cocktail consultation company Proof Drink Design. By the time you read this, you will be able to find him at his new project, Marvel Bar, in the North Loop section of downtown Minneapolis. Mr. Pip is as good as it gets. He will soon be making the Twin Cities as proud of him as I already am.

Ingredients

1¼ ounces orange or
   clementine vodka
½ ounce Lemon Sour (see p. 189)
½ ounce Campari
1½ ounces cava (approximately)

½ ounce Rosemary-Orange Syrup
   (see p. 184)
orange peel spiral
rosemary sprig

To a cobbler shaker half full of ice, add vodka, lemon sour, and Campari. Shake vigorously for 5 seconds and then strain into martini glass. Mount orange spiral on rim and top with cava. Add syrup, letting it sink to the bottom, creating a barely visible two-tone effect (the cocktail's flavor will change as one progresses through it). Finish by placing rosemary sprig on cocktail's surface.

NAME	Parma		
SPIRIT	Vodka	GLASS	Martini
CREATOR	Johnny Michaels		

Once while in Italy, I saw people snacking on platters of prosciutto and cantaloupe, and the memory inspired this drink years later. People clamor for it at the beginning of summer, but I like to wait until the cantaloupes are super sweet and juicy. This cocktail is another that's so easy I'm embarrassed to list it.

Ingredients

1½ ounces vodka

1½ ounces citrus vodka

2 ounces fresh cantaloupe juice

2 prosciutto-stuffed green olives, on a 6-inch skewer
(see instructions)

Add the liquid ingredients to a Boston tin half full of ice, swirl for a bit, and then strain into chilled martini glass. Lay skewer across the top of glass. When stuffing olives, use very thinly sliced prosciutto. I like to roll pieces up in a cone shape, stick the pointy end in the olive, and try to have the extra ham flare out in a cool way. When skewering olives, pierce near the open end, so that the bottoms hang down in the drink and the flared prosciutto points upward.

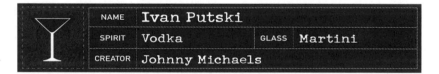

	NAME	Ivan Putski		
	SPIRIT	Vodka	GLASS	Martini
	CREATOR	Johnny Michaels		

This one is a tribute to my grandpa, who was a huge wrestling fan. I don't know what was funnier, the ridiculous WWF wrestling of the 1980s or watching Grandpa go nuts watching it. His favorite wrestler was Ivan "The Polish Power" Putski, a totally clean-cut good guy who always won and always overcame his opponents' dirty tricks. This one barely made the initial cut on the opening drink list for Café Maude but surprisingly became one of the café's most popular drinks. It's a polish potato dirty vodka martini with olives and onions and a twist or two of freshly ground black pepper.

Ingredients

4 ounces Luksusowa potato
vodka, refrigerated

½ ounce olive brine

2 green olives

2 cocktail onions

freshly ground black pepper

Swirl the liquid ingredients in a Boston tin half full of ice and then strain into cold martini glass. Alternate olives and onions on a 6-inch skewer, with an onion being closest to the tip, and submerge in drink. Finish by topping off with a twist or two of pepper.

	NAME	Margie Had Sex in the Pantry		
	SPIRIT	Vodka	GLASS	Martini
	CREATOR	Johnny Michaels		

An ex-girlfriend of mine who had moved to NYC was visiting Minneapolis with some friends, one by the name of Margie and another woman I used to play with in a local band, The Morning Stars. She had also moved to NYC and was in some ridiculously named band. We were reminiscing about crazy parties we had when we lived in this big *Addams Family*-style house of debauchery when she said that phrase, and Margie, who was sitting next to her, flashed her some dagger eyes, which made it extra funny. I then told my ex-bandmate that if she wanted a truly weird band name that would attract attention, she should name it Margie Had Sex in the Pantry and curious New Yorkers would show up to see what kind of band would give themselves such a *Fargo*-esque name. I told her they should all wear 1950s housewives' dresses and aprons while they played. And the more I thought about it, the more I thought it would make a good drink name, like an Ole and Lena joke in the form of a cocktail.

I use vodka with vanilla, maple, cardamom, and cream, all very Minnesotan. I even went so far as to use metal plumber's banding to fashion a cursive M-shaped cookie cutter that had a little hook at the top corner of the M so that the cookie could hang from the lip of the glass. I made sturdy sugar cookies with it and then frosted them with royal icing, sealing the cookie so that it wouldn't get soggy and fall off the glass. One side was light blue, and the other, light yellow, the same colors as the Swedish flag—took two days to frost those suckers! Looking back, I cannot believe I went through so much trouble making this garnish. I've always liked hanging out with FoodCookers, though.

Ingredients

2½ to 3 ounces vanilla vodka

½ ounce Grade B maple syrup (cheaper and with more maple flavor)

1 ounce half-and-half

2 to 3 dashes Cardamom Tincture (see p. 196)

Shake the liquid ingredients vigorously in a Boston shaker with not that much ice, maybe 25 percent full, 7 to 10 seconds. I like to get it nice and frothy. Strain into martini glass. Forget about making the cookie garnish, unless you just did a fat line of meth.

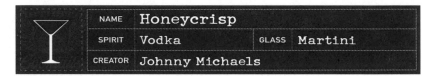

	NAME	Honeycrisp		
	SPIRIT	Vodka	GLASS	Martini
	CREATOR	Johnny Michaels		

Yeah, I know all the coolie mixologists hate appletinis, so go ahead and resume the stone casting. But there are a lot of people out there who love them (at least here in the Midwest), so I try to make them as best I can. I draw the line at the neon-green ones, though. I make mine tan and red, like Honeycrisps, but still, if I ever go to Tales of the Cocktail in New Orleans, they'll probably burn me at the stake.

Ingredients

1¾ ounces Smirnoff green apple vodka

1¼ ounces fresh apple cider

2 ounces cava (approximately)

2 to 3 dashes unsweetened pomegranate juice

apple slice

To a cobbler shaker half full of ice, add vodka and cider. Swirl for a bit (the cider should be cold already, so you don't need to chill as long as normal) and strain into martini glass. Top with cava and then add pomegranate juice (I use a 12-ounce squirt bottle with one-quarter of the tip cut off). Mount apple slice on rim at a 45-degree angle.

Jackpot

Same as the Honeycrisp, except we put a small notch, or slit, on the top side of the mounted apple slice garnish and set a scratch-off lottery ticket in it. People said we would get in trouble for doing that. I always maintained we'd be lucky if we did, because we'd stop doing it before getting fined and take the free publicity. Nothing ever came of it. Every week or so I'd have to go to the gas station, however, and buy fifty scratch-off lottery tickets, cash only, and have the other customers waiting in line looking at me as if I were a complete moron.

NAME	Dirty Apple Picker		
SPIRIT	Vodka	GLASS	Martini
CREATOR	Johnny Michaels		

This variation on the Honeycrisp is named after my right-hand man at La Belle Vie, Michael Rasmussen, who has a strange obsession with picking apples for minimum wage every fall, and sleeping in cramped cabins with ten other guys . . . and he's from Apple Valley, too.

Ingredients

1¾ ounces Smirnoff green apple vodka

1¼ ounces fresh apple cider

½ teaspoon Monin organic caramel syrup

2 ounces cava (approximately)

2 to 3 dashes unsweetened pomegranate juice

2 blue cheese–stuffed grapes, on a 6-inch skewer (see
   instructions)

To a cobbler shaker half full of ice, add vodka, cider, and syrup. Swirl for a bit and strain into martini glass. Top with cava and then add pomegranate juice. For the garnish, take 2 large, seedless green grapes, cut stem-side tips off, and bore them out by hand with a 3/8-inch drill bit (for real). Stuff with blue cheese, skewer, and suspend across top of drink.

	NAME	The Fabergé		
▽	SPIRIT	Vodka	GLASS	Martini
	CREATOR	Johnny Michaels		

Back in Mr. Pip's early days, he had a drink name idea—The Fabergé Egg. I remember tsk-tsking him and telling him he was close, and that's how The Fabergé got its name. It became my first Easter cocktail. This one is very springy and is half vodka, half gin. It's a great gateway cocktail for people who think they don't like gin. It's like a light with a dimmer switch; it doesn't have to be all on or all off. Come on, here . . . let me show you how to smoke it right.

Ingredients

1½ ounces citrus vodka
1½ ounces gin
⅓ ounce crème de violette
½ ounce Lemon Sour (see p. 189)
lemon wedge
lemon peel spiral
piece gold foil (see below)

Into a cobbler shaker full of ice, squeeze and add lemon wedge and then add the liquid ingredients. Cap, shake vigorously, and double strain into martini glass. Hang lemon spiral from rim and float gold foil on surface.

Dealing with Gold Foil

For the gold foil garnish, carefully peel back protective paper from foil pack and scrape up around 1/6 of a page with the pointy tip of a skewer. This is very tricky because it's so delicate. You want to get the foil to stand up on the drink's surface, instead of collapsing flat. The stuff is streaky, and trying harder or less hard doesn't seem to help. Sometimes the foil will stand up and hold what seems to be a physically impossible pose, like a little floating sculpture. Sometimes it collapses after a couple seconds, and sometimes it stays that way . . . "Witch!"

VODKA

NORTH STAR COCKTAILS

NAME	Mistletoe		
SPIRIT	Vodka	GLASS	Martini
CREATOR	Johnny Michaels		

This was our first Christmas specialty cocktail and is still ridiculously popular. People try to order it in the middle of summer, but it's only available from the day after Thanksgiving through New Year's Eve. It's a very attractive cocktail, although I'm a Grinch Nog man, myself (see p. 135).

Ingredients

½ ounce clementine or orange vodka

½ ounce citrus vodka

½ ounce gin

⅓ ounce unsweetened pomegranate juice

⅓ ounce Lemon Sour (see p. 189)

⅓ ounce Cointreau or triple sec

lime wedge

simple syrup (see p. 181)

dash orange bitters

3 drops orange flower water

1½ to 2 ounces cava (approximately)

Festivus Sugar (red, white, and green large-grained sanding sugar, combined)

6 to 11 fresh pomegranate seeds

orange peel spiral

Use a lime wedge dipped in simple syrup to paint half the outside rim of martini glass and then roll it in Festivus Sugar. To a cobbler shaker one-third full of ice, add all the liquid ingredients except cava. Cap and shake vigorously 5 seconds. Strain into glass, add pomegranate seeds, and hang orange spiral on rim. Top with cava last so that seeds and twist won't mar the light cava foam on the drink's surface.

VODKA

NORTH STAR COCKTAILS

Painting the outside lip of a double rocks glass with simple syrup

Rolling outside lip of double rocks glass in kosher salt

Properly rimmed double rocks glass

NAME	Black Pearl		
SPIRIT	Vodka	GLASS	Martini
CREATOR	Johnny Michaels		

I originally made this drink for Café Maude in South Minneapolis, which I helped open. It proved so popular that I moved it over to La Belle Vie, where I renamed it and it continues to be a hot seller—another vodka-based favorite for the peoples.

Ingredients

1½ ounce vodka
¾ ounce Monin blackberry syrup
¾ ounce Lime Sour (see p. 189)
1 ounce egg whites
2 dashes orange bitters

4 drops orange flower water
1½ ounces cava (approximately)
key lime wheel
1 Black Pearl Garnish, on a
    6-inch skewer (see below)

Add all liquid ingredients, except cava, to an empty Boston shaker and shake 6 to 7 seconds. Add some ice and shake vigorously another 5 seconds. Strain into martini glass and top with cava. Mount key lime on rim and place skewered candy across top of glass.

Black Pearl Garnish

I buy bags of Haribo raspberry and blackberry gummy candies. It's like playing the slots. There are on average two-thirds raspberry to one-third blackberry candies per bag. I harvest the black ones and feed the red ones to the FoodCookers.

Ingredients
Haribo blackberry candies

Gin

Nu Silver Luster Dust

Put candies in a plastic container without too much extra room in it. Add a splash of gin, cap it, and carefully shake, coating candies as lightly as possible. Try not to soak them, because doing so increases the likelihood of jet-black candy dye sneaking out of the container and staining your shirt. Drain excess liquid and transfer candies to a clean, dry container. Sprinkle Luster Dust into container. Cap and shake thoroughly and then pour out the silver-grey-black pearls onto a cookie sheet to dry cure at room temperature overnight. Store in an airtight container to keep fresh.

	NAME	Night of the Hunter		
	SPIRIT	Vodka	GLASS	Martini
	CREATOR	Johnny Michaels		

This drink is named after a cool old movie starring Robert Mitchum. It apparently took the bribe of a case of whiskey before he agreed to do it, which I find funny. This one is a rare bird, a vodka martini with some flavor complexity, thanks to the oloroso sherry. I use Ketel One or Phillips Prairie Organic vodka because I like the rich body they have. It holds the sweetness well.

This was the first time I successfully used salt solution in a drink. The black pepper–infused Cîroc vodka, pinot noir grape juice, and French grey sea salt cocktail recipe that I was convinced would be awesome sucked royal. This drink was inspired by Adrianne Odom's Salty Carmel ice cream that she had on the dessert menu when

La Belle Vie first relocated to Minneapolis in 2005. Once I made this drink, I was one happy, blind squirrel, and it got me thinking (people were always asking where that grinding noise was coming from). I use salt solution in a lot of cocktails and pre-mixes, and most of the time I try to keep it low, quiet, practically imperceptible. I use it to enhance flavors but not necessarily to be salty. I keep mine in a squirt bottle in my bitters and tinctures collection. I use kosher salt, but any noniodized salt would work. I thought about making an MSG solution to see what that would be like, but I just couldn't bring myself to do it. I figured I'm already going to be eternally spanked by bar spoons after I kick the bucket, and I don't need some demon squirting me in the eye with an MSG tincture on top of that.

Ingredients

4 ounces Ketel One vodka
½ ounce Night of the Hunter Mix (see below)
2 Marcona almond–stuffed green olives, on a 6-inch skewer
    (see below)

To a Boston tin with plenty of ice, add liquids and swirl or stir with instrument of choice. When desired coldness and dilution is reached, say 10 seconds or so, strain into chilled martini glass. Garnish with olives submerged in drink, as opposed to laid across the top. One can adjust the amount of Night of the Hunter Mix to suit personal taste.

Stuffing Olives

When stuffing Marcona almonds into olives, slightly pinch the olives so that their round opening becomes more oval to match the Marconas, which are flatter than traditional almonds. You will get less olive splitting this way. To skewer them, take a stuffed olive, pierce its flesh so that the skewer's tip hits the flat side of the almond, and then gently but firmly tap the olive on a flat surface, not your hand (we are not trying to skewer you). This should help the skewer pierce the almond cleanly without breaking it up. If your olives continually break, prestuff them a little bit ahead of time to soften the almond (but not days ahead of time, for the almonds will lose their crunch).

Skewering almond-stuffed green olives

Night of the Hunter Mix

Licor 43 is a Spanish liqueur that supposedly has forty-three herbs and spices in it but tastes like vanilla syrup to me. Sherries can be either super sweet or dry, and olorosos are a notch down from the sweetest, generally speaking. The sherry is where the cocktail's wall of magic flavor comes from. The measurement is approximate because, as unpredictable as wine, sherries vary from producer to producer. I start off with this two-to-one blend of Licor 43 to oloroso, taste, and then adjust until I get the caramel taste I'm after. Then I add the salt solution until the mix tastes slightly too salty. When cut with vodka, the salt flavor drops down into proper balance for some reason unknown to me.

Ingredients
2 ounces Licor 43
1 ounce oloroso sherry (approximately)
salt solution (see p. 31)

Mix Licor 43 and sherry and adjust to taste. Add salt solution. Start with 1 dash and work your way up. Makes enough for 5 or 6 cocktails.

	NAME	Valentino		
	SPIRIT	Vodka	GLASS	Martini
	CREATOR	Johnny Michaels		

This was our first Valentine's drink at La Belle Vie. I needed a pomegranate cocktail (give me break, it was 2006) to replace our holiday Mistletoe martini. This one is so popular that it stays on the list eleven months a year and only comes off from Thanksgiving through New Year's Eve (and then I hear the howling).

Shake this one vigorously to soften the sweet liquor and premix combo and to make it a bit frothy. The less ice you use, the frothier the cocktail will be. Mount the orange twist before topping off the drink with cava because doing it afterward will result in a bald spot in the fine layer of cava foam. It eventually disappears, but why not do it right?

Ingredients

1½ ounces clementine or orange vodka
1½ ounces Valentino Mix (see below)
2 ounces cava (approximately)
orange peel spiral
candied ginger, on a 6-inch skewer

To a cobbler shaker one-third full of ice, add vodka and Valentino Mix. Cap and shake vigorously 5 seconds or so. Strain into martini glass and garnish with orange spiral. Top with cava and lay skewered ginger across top of glass.

Valentino Mix
Ingredients

4 ounces Ginger Syrup (see p. 182)
4 ounces unsweetened pomegranate juice
½ teaspoon orange bitters

Mix and store in a 12-ounce squirt bottle. Makes enough for about 6 cocktails.

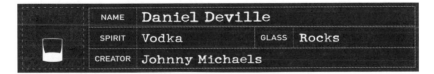

	NAME	To Die with Music		
	SPIRIT	Vodka	GLASS	Double shot
	CREATOR	Johnny Michaels		

I recently heard this Russian phrase, which means to go out with gusto. What a drink name! The ideal liquor to use for this would be Nemiroff Ukrainian honey-pepper vodka. It's not easy to find in Minnesota, so I blend Russian honey with Russian vodka. You can also serve this one in a 2½-ounce clear-glass votive candleholder. Don't laugh. They make great mini-glasses.

Ingredients

16 ounces Stolichnaya vodka
4 ounces Russian honey (regular honey would be fine)
2 ounces Siberian ginseng extract (Korean Ginseng extract
   would be fine)
½ ounce (add more to taste) Hot Pepper Tincture (see p. 195)

Microwave honey until runny, add vodka, and mix well. Add ginseng and Hot Pepper Tincture, mix again, and funnel into a bottle. Store in refrigerator or freezer and serve cold in double shot glass. Shake bottle before serving.

79

	NAME	Daniel Deville		
	SPIRIT	Vodka	GLASS	Rocks
	CREATOR	Johnny Michaels		

This drink pulled me off the wagon the first time I had been on it for over a year. La Belle Vie had just opened, and I had never tasted cream sherries before. So amazing, so condensed. When I added vodka to it, it was almost like zooming out, and my unrefined palate could see it, taste it better. This drink is just a more complex Black Russian.

This sharp-dressed Korean dude used to come into La Belle Vie when we first opened. He was from NYC, doing some consulting work for Northwest Airlines. His wife was supposedly in the fashion industry, and he wore these super-tight plaid suits

VODKA

NORTH STAR COCKTAILS

with way-too-short sleeves and pants. I unintentionally pulled him off the wagon with this one. He apparently had quit drinking for a long time and then had slipped into just wine for a while. I didn't know this when I offered him one of these. He told me after. He then tried real hard to get me to drink one with him while I was working—so evil! He wanted to name this one Sweet Jesus because that's what he said he would wake up screaming after ending the night with a few of these. He apparently got into an argument with another patron on a night I wasn't working, and I never saw him again.

Ingredients

2 ounces Ketel One vodka
1 ounce cream sherry
3 hazelnuts, blanched

Pour liquors into rocks glass and add ice. Garnish with hazelnuts. I used to say this cocktail could only be stirred with a knife.

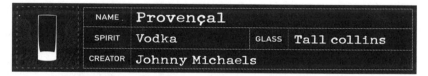

NAME	Provençal		
SPIRIT	Vodka	GLASS	Tall collins
CREATOR	Johnny Michaels		

This one's basically a vodka collins with a French twist.

Ingredients

2 ounces citrus vodka
2 ounces Provençal Syrup (see p. 185)
cold club soda
lemon wheel

Pour vodka and syrup into tall collins glass with ice and mix with a straw. Top with cold club soda, gently remix, and insert a lemon wheel.

NAME	Supernishipowa		
SPIRIT	Vodka	GLASS	Tall collins
CREATOR	Johnny Michaels		

This one's named after the Minnesota Twins' Japanese second baseman, Tsuyoshi Nishioka, whom they signed in 2011. It's the result of my quest to make a good-tasting energy drink cocktail. The secret is the Hi-Ball lemon-lime energy soda water.

Ingredients

2 ounces Cola Cherry Vodka (see below)
1 ounce Lemon Sour (see p. 189)
Hi-Ball lemon-lime energy soda water
lemon wheel
brandied cherry, on a 6-inch skewer

Fill a tall collins glass with ice and add vodka and sour. Top with energy soda water, insert lemon wheel, and garnish with skewered cherry.

Cola Cherry Vodka

Ingredients

1 liter vodka
18 ounces simple syrup (see p. 181)
1 tablespoon cola extract
1 tablespoon cherry extract
2 tablespoons salt solution (see p. 31)

Mix ingredients and store in a bottle. Makes 1½ liters.

VODKA

NORTH STAR COCKTAILS

NAME	Chloroform Kiss		
SPIRIT	Vodka	GLASS	Tall collins
CREATOR	Johnny Michaels		

We made this one up for Mike Woychek, my all-pro pulling guard offensive lineman Saturday night barback. He and Jesse Heinrichs are my two hall-of-fame barbacks, two princes. La Belle Vie and I owe them so much thanks for any success the cocktail program has enjoyed. La Belle Vie's lounge turns into a high-volume bar on busy nights, and without their all-out efforts, we wouldn't be able to pull things off. I've maintained that I will probably quit when they leave because the drop-off will be too heartbreaking. During Christmas season 2010, Mike had a broken wrist and was on the injured reserve list for ten-plus weeks. He wanted to seal his cast in plastic wrap and come to work one armed—now that's a player! Of course we wouldn't let him. You have to protect players from themselves sometimes, but that's the type of people you want on your team. Anyway, after five or six hours of washing glassware and running all over the building for this and that, Mike can develop a powerful thirst, and he likes to hit the ramp and catch some air. When he was growing up in Winona, Minnesota, he liked Long Island Iced Teas, so I came up with a Tom Collins with a sophisticated twist and the power of a Long Island. The name is fitting. I warn people who order it that it's aptly named, and then they act surprised when it hits them—and then they call the next day to see if they left their sunglasses at the bar.

Ingredients

1½ ounces citrus vodka
1½ ounces London dry gin
1 ounce Yellow Chartreuse
½ ounce Lemon Sour (see p. 189)
1½ ounces cava (approximately)
orange slice

To a tall collins glass, add all the liquid ingredients except cava. Stir with a straw, add a couple more cubes, and then top with cava. The drink should then just require a poke or two with the straw to be mixed. Garnish by inserting orange slice (do not mount on rim, please).

NAME	Tomgirl (or A Tomgirl Named Maude)		
SPIRIT	Vodka	GLASS	Tall collins
CREATOR	Johnny Michaels		

Here's another Café Maude original that I brought to La Belle Vie after it proved popular. Café Maude is in a nice residential neighborhood and was named after Maude Armitage. She apparently was a big tomboy and an early women's rights leader in the Twin Cities. I've always liked the tomboys and have had lots of crushes on women who were tomboys as girls. As for the name, "Tomgirl," I think in the stress of getting that place open, with bullets flying everywhere, my brain malfunctioned (alert the media), and I put the name down wrong on the menu. Oh, well.

I thought this simple drink with a little extra flavor would go over in the neighborhood, and it did, as well as at La Belle Vie. This drink has surprised me with its staying power. It hasn't been on our list for four years, but I still get orders for it every week.

Ingredients

1½ ounces Absolut Ruby Red vodka
½ ounce Pama pomegranate liqueur
1¼ ounces Tomgirl Mix (approximately; see below)
1¼ ounces Sprite (approximately)
1 maraschino cherry

To a tall collins glass with ice, add vodka and liqueur and stir with a straw. The ice should collapse a bit, so top with more ice. Split the remaining volume between Tomgirl Mix and Sprite. Garnish with maraschino cherry.

Tomgirl Mix

Ingredients

16 ounces unsweetened pink grapefruit juice
¾ teaspoon cayenne pepper
¾ tablespoon kosher salt

Mix ingredients and store refrigerated in a sealed container or squirt bottle.

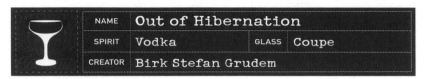

NAME	Out of Hibernation		
SPIRIT	Vodka	GLASS	Coupe
CREATOR	Birk Stefan Grudem		

Ingredients

2 ounces North Shore aquavit

½ ounce Smith & Cross rum

¼ ounce Velvet Falernum

½ ounce Cocchi Aperitivo Americano

¾ (heavy) ounce fresh lime juice

9 drops Regan's orange bitters

absinthe

orange twist

Rinse coupe with absinthe, discarding excess. Shake remaining liquid ingredients with ice and strain into coupe. Garnish with orange twist.

NAME	Stockholm Syndrome		
SPIRIT	Vodka	GLASS	Martini
CREATOR	Pip Hanson		

Make the simple syrup at a ratio of 2 parts sugar to 1 part water.

Ingredients

2 ounces Aalborg aquavit

1 ounce Tío Pepe fino sherry

1 ounce fresh lemon juice

½ ounce simple syrup

1 to 2 dashes lingonberry concentrate

lingonberry, on a 6-inch skewer

Shake all the liquid ingredients except lingonberry concentrate and strain into chilled martini glass. Sink lingonberry concentrate to bottom of glass and garnish with skewered lingonberry.

NAME	Cold Comfort		
SPIRIT	Vodka	GLASS	Rocks
CREATOR	Pip Hanson		

Ingredients

2 ounces Linie aquavit

1½ ounces Wild Turkey rye

¼ ounce Luxardo maraschino liqueur

3 dashes Peychaud's bitters

2 dashes Regan's orange bitters

dash Black Pepper Sambuca (see p. 200)

Stir all ingredients in a mixing glass with ice and strain into chilled rocks glass.

NAME	Norwegian Sunset		
SPIRIT	Vodka	GLASS	Coupe
CREATOR	Jesse Held		

Ingredients

1½ ounces Linie aquavit

¾ ounce Aperol

½ ounce Carpano Antica sweet vermouth

5 drops Regan's orange bitters

Stir all ingredients, except bitters, in a mixing glass with ice and strain into chilled coupe. Add bitters.

NAME	Square Peg		
SPIRIT	Vodka	GLASS	Rocks
CREATOR	Jesse Held		

Ingredients

1½ ounces Square One Botanical vodka

½ ounce cream sherry

¼ ounce fresh lemon juice

1 teaspoon powdered sugar

dash cherry bitters

brandied cherry, on a skewer

Shake the liquid ingredients and sugar with ice and strain into ice-filled rocks glass. Insert brandied cherry skewer.

NAME	Prairie Rose		
SPIRIT	Vodka	GLASS	Coupe
CREATOR	Gina Kent		

Ingredients

2 ounces Prairie Organic vodka

½ ounce Hazelnut Orgeat (see p. 185)

¼ ounce Grenadine (see p. 186)

¼ ounce fresh lemon juice

rosewater, in a spray bottle

Shake all ingredients, except rosewater, and strain into coupe. Top with a mist of rosewater.

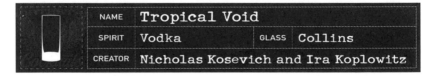

NAME	Tropical Void		
SPIRIT	Vodka	GLASS	Collins
CREATOR	Nicholas Kosevich and Ira Koplowitz		

Ingredients

1½ ounces Rehorst vodka

¾ ounce pineapple juice

½ ounce simple syrup (see p. 181)

dash Peychaud's bitters

¼ ounce fresh lime juice   orange slice

½ ounce Aperol   French cherry

Shake the liquid ingredients with ice and strain into collins glass over rocks. Garnish with orange slice and cherry.

NAME	**The King's Cup**
SPIRIT	**Vodka** **GLASS** **Double rocks**
CREATOR	**Garrett Nitzchke and Geoffrey Trelstad**

This is our take on the British cocktail of sport, the Pimm's Cup.

Ingredients

1½ ounces Cucumber Vodka   club soda

(see p. 203)   7Up

¾ ounce Pimm's   cucumber spear

¾ ounce Lemon Sour (see p. 189)   lemon wheel

Pour vodka, Pimm's, and sour into double rocks glass, stir, and fill with ice. Top with club soda and 7Up. Garnish with cucumber spear, lemon wheel, and a sipping straw.

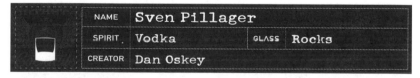

NAME	**Sven Pillager**
SPIRIT	**Vodka** **GLASS** **Rocks**
CREATOR	**Dan Oskey**

Ingredients

2 ounces Linie aquavit

½ ounce Cynar

1 teaspoon Rosemary-Maple Syrup (see p. 187)

4 dashes Black Walnut Bitters (see p. 194)

orange wheel

Shake all the liquid ingredients, except bitters, with ice and pour contents into rocks glass. Top with bitters and garnish with orange wheel.

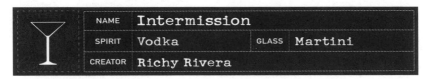

Ingredients

1½ ounces vodka

1 ounce Pama pomegranate
liqueur

1 ounce Pomegranate-Lavender
Syrup (see p. 188)

splash cranberry juice

lemon wedge

Lavender Sugar (see below)

lemon twist

Rub martini glass rim with lemon wedge and coat with Lavender Sugar. Shake the liquid ingredients with ice and strain into glass. Garnish with lemon twist.

Lavender Sugar

Ingredients

2 cups sugar

½ cup culinary lavender buds

Mix in a food processor. Sift sugar mixture in a sifter or in a bowl with a whisk. Store in an airtight container.

NAME **Spring Gimlet**

SPIRIT Vodka　　GLASS Collins

CREATOR Richy Rivera

Ingredients

1½ ounces Tito's vodka

1 ounce Ginger-Rosemary Syrup
(see p. 188)

1 lime, juiced

lime wheel

rosemary sprig

Shake vodka, syrup, and lime juice with ice and strain into ice-filled collins glass. Garnish with lime wheel and rosemary sprig.

NAME	Cucumber-Melon-Infused Martini
SPIRIT	Vodka
GLASS	Martini
CREATOR	Christa Robinson

I always make infusions in glass and refrigerate them. Ketel One vodka has always infused the best for me. When making the infusion, the ratio by volume should roughly be 2 parts vodka to 1 part cucumber and melon.

Ingredients

1 liter Ketel One vodka

1 cucumber, peeled, seeded, and sliced

1 wedge honeydew melon, peeled and chopped

1 wedge cantaloupe, peeled and chopped

cucumber slice or melon sorbet

Combine vodka, cucumber, and melons in a glass jar and seal. Refrigerate 3 to 4 weeks and strain. Store in refrigerator. To serve, pour into martini glass and garnish with a slice of cucumber or a small scoop of melon sorbet.

NAME	Norwegian Ginger
SPIRIT	Vodka
GLASS	Rocks
CREATOR	Peder Schweigert

Ingredients

2 ounces North Shore aquavit

3 ounces Ginger Beer (see p. 205)

¼ ounce cherry liqueur

1 eyedropper Bittercube Jamaican #2 bitters

To an ice-filled rocks glass, add, in order, aquavit, ginger beer, cherry liqueur, and bitters.

Tequila

NAME	Enter the Dragon		
SPIRIT	Tequila	GLASS	Tall collins
CREATOR	Johnny Michaels		

Every now and then, when you're psychically panhandling for ideas, a twenty-dollar bill lands in your hat. I love those fleeting moments of temporary self-satisfaction, and I got one of those when this name and drink combo came to me. Not sure how the name arrived. I think I had seen a part of a Bruce Lee documentary recently, and the shreds of red Fresno pepper floating in the drink reminded me of the movie poster, where he's got those cuts all over him.

Ingredients

2 ounces reposado tequila

2½ ounces Dragon Mix (see below)

2 to 3 fresh red Fresno pepper slices, seeded

lime wedge

2 ounces cava (approximately)

½ sugar, ½ kosher salt mixture

orange slice

key lime wheel

Rub lime wedge around half a tall collins glass rim and coat with sugar-salt mixture. In an empty pint glass, add pepper slices and muddle—pulverize—with a flat-bottomed wooden muddler until pulpy. Add lime wedge, muddle that, and then add tequila and Dragon Mix. Swirl around to loosen fruit. Pour contents into ice-filled glass. Add a few more ice cubes and top with cava. Insert orange and key lime.

Seeding red Fresno peppers

Dragon Mix

Ingredients

1 cup Boiron passion fruit purée, defrosted

¼ cup Cointreau or triple sec

1 cup simple syrup (see p. 181)

2½ ounces pulp-free orange juice concentrate, defrosted

½ teaspoon orange bitters

Mix ingredients and store in a 24-ounce squirt bottle. Makes enough for 7 or 8 cocktails.

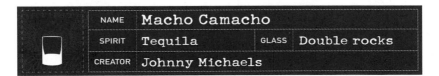

NAME	Macho Camacho		
SPIRIT	Tequila	GLASS	Double rocks
CREATOR	Johnny Michaels		

I dig this one and am surprised no tequila company has stolen the idea by now. I infuse silver tequila with ancho pepper powder. It gives the tequila a deep-red color and a great flavor without too much heat.

Ingredients

2 ounces Ancho Tequila (see p. 199)

2 ounces Macho Camacho Mix (see below)

2 ounces cava (approximately)

lime wedge

kosher salt

key lime wheel

orange or blood orange slice

Rub lime wedge around half a double rocks glass rim and coat with kosher salt. To a pint glass full of ice, add tequila, Macho Camacho Mix, and squeezed lime wedge. Cap and shake on medium 4 to 5 seconds. Pour into glass and top with cava. Stir and garnish with key lime and orange.

Macho Camacho Mix

Ingredients

5 ounces orange juice concentrate, defrosted

5 ounces Monin blood orange syrup

½ teaspoon orange bitters

Mix ingredients and store in a 12-ounce squirt bottle. Makes enough for 5 cocktails.

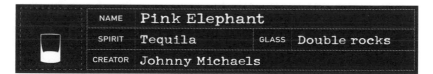

	NAME	Pink Elephant		
	SPIRIT	Tequila	GLASS	Double rocks
	CREATOR	Johnny Michaels		

When I first added this drink to the La Belle Vie list, I called it I'll Bet You Do, some vague but suggestive song lyric I heard, but after a while, I didn't like it. Then, I remembered the old party house I lived in, the one that looked like the *Addams Family* mansion. When I lived there, I cemented an awesome two-foot-tall gargoyle right in the middle of the stairs leading up from the sidewalk, and then I flanked him on both sides with plastic pink elephant lawn ornaments. (Check out my author photo. I can't believe the Minnesota Historical Society let me have him in the photo.

I recently learned that gargoyles are protectors and I've begun collecting them. There are now several in my apartment, but this one will always be my favorite.) Anyway, I changed the name to Pink Elephant—a great spring margarita.

Ingredients

1½ ounces silver tequila

½ ounce Cointreau

½ ounce Aperol

¾ ounce fresh pink grapefruit juice

¾ ounce Lime Sour (see p. 189)

2 lime wedges

kosher salt

key lime wheel

blood orange or orange slice (optional)

Rub one of the lime wedges around half a double rocks glass rim and coat with kosher salt. Into a Boston shaker filled with ice, squeeze and add remaining lime wedge and then add the liquid ingredients. Cap and shake well 6 seconds or so. Pour contents into glass. Mount key lime on rim or just lay flat on surface. Insert optional orange slice.

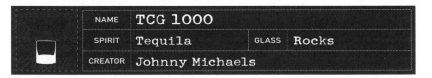

NAME	TCG 1000		
SPIRIT	Tequila	GLASS	Rocks
CREATOR	Johnny Michaels		

So I decided to use a few car-sounding names, before moving on to spacecraft. (What? You think they don't have model names, too? Just wait.) This one stands for Tequila Cucumber Gimlet. I premixed this one at La Belle Vie but will break it down for you. If you like it, commit to making a whole bottle, especially in a party situation. It'll stay good refrigerated at least a week, probably two.

Ingredients

2 ounces Cucumber Tequila (see p. 199)

¾ ounce Lime Sour (see p. 189)

1 teaspoon Black Pepper Syrup (see p. 184)

3 dashes salt solution (see p. 31)

lime wedge

key lime slice

cucumber slice

2 or 3 blanched hazelnuts (optional)

Into a pint glass two-thirds full of ice, squeeze and add lime wedge and then add all the liquid ingredients. Cap and shake vigorously 6 to 7 seconds. Pour contents into rocks glass. Lay key lime slice and cucumber slice on surface. Insert optional hazelnuts.

NAME	Godzillita!!! Attack From Above!!!		
SPIRIT	Tequila	GLASS	Double rocks
CREATOR	Johnny Michaels		

A spicy plum margarita. I just had a gut feeling about this one. In my head it took some tracking, some fine tuning, but I hunted it down and got it. I renamed it Attack from Above for La Belle Vie (a little role reversal here: that's a band name I might use someday). I walked through the biggest Asian food store in the Twin Cities three times, aisle by aisle, slow foot by slow foot (watched by security cameras the whole time, I'm sure), looking for something new, some interesting and great ingredient I didn't know about, and this plum tea syrup I found just rocks. Extra tasty!

Ingredients

2 ounces reposado tequila

2 ounces Godzillita Mix (see below)

lime wedge

$\frac{1}{2}$ black salt, $\frac{1}{2}$ kosher salt mixture

key lime wheel

tapioca pearls (optional)

Rub lime wedge around half a double rocks glass rim and coat with salt mixture. To a pint glass full of ice, add the liquid ingredients, cap, and powershake 4 to 5 seconds. Pour contents into double rocks glass. Garnish with key lime wheel and optional tapioca pearls (depends how psychedelic you want it).

Godzillita Mix

Ingredients

3 ounces Assi plum tea syrup (distributed by Rhee Bros.)

3 ounces Ginger Syrup (see p. 182)

3 ounces fresh lemon juice

1 tablespoon white vinegar

1 tablespoon salt solution (see p. 31)

1 teaspoon Hot Pepper Tincture (see p. 195)

1 to 2 drops mesquite smoke extract

1 to 2 drops green food coloring

Mix and store in a 12-ounce squirt bottle or sealed container.

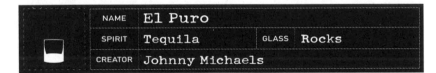

	NAME	El Puro		
	SPIRIT	Tequila	GLASS	Rocks
	CREATOR	Johnny Michaels		

This drink is the 2.0 version of something I created for a tequila bar a few years ago. It's very simple, just seasoning a good-quality reposado tequila. I pride myself on making a lot of drinks people seem to really like that use best-value spirits, and often great base spirits can be found in the ten- to fifteen-dollar price range. This drink requires a little higher-quality base spirit, however, because it really is the star of the show, with everything else just used to accent it. I've also yet to find a great ten-dollar bottle of tequila.

At La Belle Vie I premix everything together, pour it back in the original tequila bottle, and then store it in the refrigerator. If you try and love this drink and want to commit to a whole bottle, that's how I would recommend preparing it. I have modified my recipe here for an individual cocktail, so you may need to taste and adjust the initial, prechilling mixture to personal preference. Take care, though, to under- rather than overdo it, or you will be adding more and more tequila to compensate. Remember, everything but the tequila is supposed to be barely perceptible.

Ingredients

2½ ounces Herradura reposado tequila

½ ounce dark-amber agave nectar

1 to 2 dashes citric acid solution (see below)

2 dashes salt solution (see p. 31)

1 to 2 dashes Hot Pepper Tincture (see p. 195)

1 or 3 thin slices apple (I prefer Honeycrisp)

Mix the liquid ingredients in a pint glass with a spoon to blend agave nectar. Transfer mixture to a Boston shaker with no ice and place in freezer 15 minutes or so. Add ice to shaker and shake. Pour contents into rocks glass and insert apple slice(s). No straw.

Citric Acid Solution

Ingredients

1 ounce citric acid powder

3 ounces water

Mix and store in an eyedropper bottle.

	NAME	Cobra Verde		
	SPIRIT	Tequila	GLASS	Double rocks
	CREATOR	Johnny Michaels		

A traditional margarita has the flavors of lime and orange. This one has lime and cherry. While there is salt on half the rim, there is also salt solution and absinthe in the drink, too, which give it a gaminess that I like. That is one of my favorite flavor trios, citrus-salt-anise.

Ingredients

2 ounces reposado tequila

½ ounce maraschino liqueur

2 lime wedges

kosher salt

1 ounce Lime Sour (see p. 189)   key lime wheel
½ ounce egg white (optional)   3 hazelnuts, blanched
heavy dash absinthe or Pernod   brandied cherry, on a 6-inch
dash salt solution (see p. 31)   skewer

Rub one of the lime wedges around half a double rocks glass rim and coat with kosher salt. Into a pint glass filled with ice, squeeze and add remaining lime wedge and then add the liquid ingredients. Cap and powershake 6 to 7 seconds. Pour contents into glass. Float key lime wheel and hazelnuts on drink's surface. Insert skewered cherry so that cherry just sticks out of drink's surface.

NAME	Morricone		
SPIRIT	Tequila	GLASS	Rocks
CREATOR	Pip Hanson		

Ingredients

1½ ounces Don Julio añejo   dash orange bitters
   tequila   1 teaspoon Cacao Nib Mezcal
1½ ounces Campari   (see p. 201)

Build drink in order given over large pieces of ice in rocks glass.

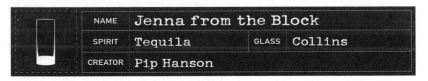

NAME	Jenna from the Block		
SPIRIT	Tequila	GLASS	Collins
CREATOR	Pip Hanson		

Ingredients

2 ounces Sauza Hornitos plata tequila
3 to 6 slices Fresno pepper
lime wedge   1 ounce pineapple juice
lemon wedge   Reed's Extra Ginger Brew

Add pepper to collins glass and muddle. Squeeze and add lemon and lime and then add tequila. Muddle again briefly, then add ice and pineapple juice, and top with ginger brew. Stir gently.

NAME	Sister Tristessa		
SPIRIT	Tequila	GLASS	Martini
CREATOR	Pip Hanson		

Ingredients

1½ ounces Sauza Hornitos reposado tequila

1½ ounces Noilly Prat dry vermouth

½ ounce simple syrup (see p. 181)

1 ounce fresh lemon juice

6 cucumber slices

Muddle 5 cucumber slices and tequila at the bottom of a shaker. Add remaining ingredients and shake hard. Strain with a Hawthorn strainer and a fine-mesh strainer into chilled martini glass. Float remaining cucumber slice.

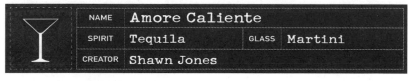

NAME	Ponce de Leon		
SPIRIT	Tequila	GLASS	Collins
CREATOR	Jesse Held		

Ingredients

2 ounces Lemongrass-Ginger Tequila (see p. 201)

¼ (heavy) ounce crème de mûre

3 lime wedges

3 ounces ginger beer

lime wheel

Muddle lime wedges in bottom of collins glass. Add ice, tequila, and ginger beer nearly to the top. Drop in crème de mûre for effect. Garnish with lime wheel.

NAME	Amore Caliente		
SPIRIT	Tequila	GLASS	Martini
CREATOR	Shawn Jones		

Ingredients

2 ounces Jalapeño Tequila (see p. 202)

1 ounce Cointreau

Muddling limes

1 ounce fresh lime juice

½ ounce Monin pomegranate syrup

½ ounce Monin passion fruit syrup

lime wedge

½ black salt, ½ sea salt mixture

8 drops Bittercube orange bitters

Rub lime wedge around rim of martini glass and coat with salt mixture. Shake all the liquid ingredients, except bitters, and strain into glass. Add bitters around rim.

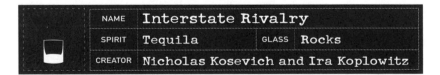

	NAME	Interstate Rivalry		
	SPIRIT	Tequila	GLASS	Rocks
	CREATOR	Nicholas Kosevich and Ira Koplowitz		

Ingredients

1½ ounces Partida blanco tequila

½ ounce Del Maguey Santo Domingo mezcal

¼ ounce agave nectar

$\frac{3}{4}$ dropper Bittercube Bolívar bitters

$\frac{1}{2}$ dropper Bittercube cherry bark–vanilla bitters

orange peel coin

Stir the liquid ingredients with ice and strain into ice-filled rocks glass. Squeeze orange coin over drink to express oils and drop in.

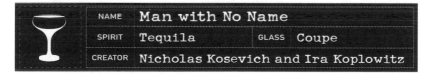

	NAME	Forgotten Connection		
	SPIRIT	Tequila	GLASS	Coupe
	CREATOR	Nicholas Kosevich and Ira Koplowitz		

Ingredients

$1\frac{3}{4}$ ounces Cazadores reposado tequila

$\frac{1}{2}$ ounce Amaro Nonino

$\frac{1}{4}$ (heavy) ounce Frangelico

dash Peychaud's bitters

lemon peel coin, notched

Stir the liquid ingredients in a mixing glass with ice and strain into coupe. Squeeze lemon peel over drink and hang on coupe by notch.

	NAME	Man with No Name		
	SPIRIT	Tequila	GLASS	Coupe
	CREATOR	Nicholas Kosevich and Ira Koplowitz		

Ingredients

$1\frac{1}{2}$ ounces Cazadores reposado tequila

$\frac{1}{4}$ ounce Cointreau

$\frac{1}{3}$ ounce Green Chartreuse

$\frac{3}{4}$ ounce fresh lemon juice

$\frac{1}{2}$ ounce simple syrup (see p. 181)

17 drops Bittercube cherry bark–vanilla bitters

5 drops Coriander Tincture (see p. 197)

Shake all ingredients except tincture in a shaker with ice and strain into coupe. Garnish with tincture.

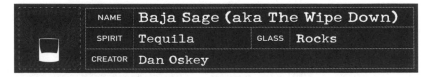

NAME	Baja Sage (aka The Wipe Down)		
SPIRIT	Tequila	GLASS	Rocks
CREATOR	Dan Oskey		

Make the honey syrup by dissolving 1 part honey in 1 part boiling water.

Ingredients

2 ounces Roasted-Sweet Corn Tequila (see p. 203)

¼ ounce Domaine de Canton ginger liqueur

1 teaspoon honey syrup   3 to 4 fresh sage leaves

½ lime, juiced   lime wedge

In a mixing glass, muddle sage, lime juice, and syrup. Fill with ice and add tequila and liqueur. Shake and pour contents into rocks glass. Garnish with lime wedge.

NAME	Mango Margarita		
SPIRIT	Tequila	GLASS	Double rocks
CREATOR	Christa Robinson		

This cocktail was developed for Rainbow Chinese, and I also put it on the menu at King & I Thai. It's important to understand when to take the time and energy to create a cocktail component from scratch. Using fresh citrus for the sour mix in a margarita is essential. But there are great products out there, like mango purée, that store easily and improve consistency when re-creating drinks in a restaurant setting.

Ingredients

1¾ ounces Sauza Hornitos plata   1 ounce mango purée
tequila   2 lime wedges

½ ounce Cointreau   kosher salt

½ ounce fresh lemon juice   lime wheel
½ ounce fresh lime juice   2 or 3 hazelnuts
1 ounce simple syrup (see p. 181)

Rub one of the lime wedges around the rim of a chilled double rocks glass and coat with salt. Shake liquid ingredients and mango purée with ice and strain into ice-filled glass. Squeeze and drop in remaining lime wedge. Garnish with lime wheel and hazelnuts.

NAME	His Majesty's Request		
SPIRIT	Tequila	GLASS	Martini
CREATOR	Sonya Runkle and Geoffrey Trelstad		

This tequila old-fashioned was inspired by Fee Brothers whiskey barrel–aged bitters.

Ingredients

3 ounces Sauza Conmemorativo añejo tequila
½ ounce simple syrup (see p. 181)
3 drops Fee Brothers whiskey barrel–aged bitters
orange peel coin, flamed (see below)
orange twist

To a mixing glass filled with ice, add the liquid ingredients and stir. Let sit 1 minute and strain into chilled martini glass. Flame orange coin over drink and garnish with orange twist.

Flaming a Citrus Peel

For this technique, you want a thick, coin-shaped slice of orange peel. The thick middle pith will keep the coin from breaking in two. Hold it a couple inches above the cocktail, between thumb and forefinger. Use a lighter instead of a match; they're easier to use, and it takes less time. With your lit lighter between cocktail and orange coin, pinch coin, skin side facing cocktail, releasing the citrus oils, which will flare brilliantly, if you have the knack, anyway. And I don't care what the hell you're doing, but I hope you have the knack.

NAME	**Black Orchid**		
SPIRIT	Tequila	GLASS	Hurricane
CREATOR	Geoffrey Trelstad		

Ingredients

1½ ounces Patrón XO Café coffee-tequila liqueur

½ ounce Godiva chocolate liqueur

½ ounce Baileys Irish cream

iced coffee

whipped cream

shaved chocolate

3 coffee beans

To a hurricane glass filled with ice, add coffee and chocolate liqueurs. Fill with iced coffee, leaving room at the top for garnish, and top with Baileys. Garnish with whipped cream, shaved chocolate, and coffee beans. Insert straw and serve.

Rum

NAME	**Kill Devil**	
SPIRIT	Rum	GLASS **Shot**
CREATOR	**Johnny Michaels**	

I made this one up for Smalley's Caribbean Barbeque and Pirate Bar in Stillwater, Minnesota. Shawn Smalley was the original MeatCooker/GrillMan at La Belle Vie when it moved from Stillwater to Minneapolis. He was born, raised, and still lives there. He looks (and drinks) like a pirate, has a huge black beard, and plays guitar in a death metal band. Most of the drinks I did for them were aimed at the tourists and such who flock to the town all summer to go boating on the St. Croix River or antiquing—accessible crowd pleasers, punches and mojitos. But this is what a real pirate would drink if he walked in there. The locals are beer and shot lovers, so it was for them, too.

Keep this one in a dark, 750-milliliter port bottle with the original label soaked off and replaced with a long piece of masking tape wrapped around the bottle a couple times, with "Kill Devil" and "XXX" written in black marker. A cork is used as the bottle's stopper. Store it in the freezer, and serve it in small, thick, old-school shot glasses.

Ingredients

9 ounces Gosling's Black Seal rum

10 ounces Bacardi 151 rum

3½ ounces Monin organic caramel syrup

½ ounce Angostura bitters

½ ounce Fee Brothers old-fashioned bitters

½ ounce Fee Brothers orange bitters

1 ounce salt solution (see p. 31)

Mix all ingredients, funnel into port bottle, and cap with cork. Store in freezer and serve in shot glasses.

NAME	Cortez the Killer		
SPIRIT	Rum	GLASS	Double rocks
CREATOR	Johnny Michaels		

This drink is named after one of my all-time favorite songs, first as Neil Young's original and then as Built to Spill's epic cover. It's an extra-strong sparkling sangria. I was happy to marry the name to the cocktail; they make a beautiful couple. The secret is the red wine reduction, which gives the drink its tannic, dry flavor and body, but then it's jazzed up by the sparkling wine and powered by its rum and liqueur base— a killer indeed.

Ingredients

2 ounces Mount Gay Eclipse gold rum

1½ ounces Cortez the Killer Mix (see below)

1½ ounces cava

orange slice

2 sliced grapes

brandied cherry, on a 6-inch skewer

Fill a double rocks glass with ice and add rum and then Cortez mix. Mix with a straw, top with cava, and garnish with orange, sliced grapes, and skewered cherry.

Cortez the Killer Mix

Ingredients

8 ounces full-bodied red wine (cabernet sauvignon, zinfandel, whatever), reduced to 2 ounces

2 ounces orange juice concentrate, defrosted

3 ounces maraschino liqueur

2 ounces apricot liqueur

Mix ingredients and store in a 12-ounce squirt bottle. This batch will make enough for 6 cocktails. Will keep refrigerated at least a week (probably way longer).

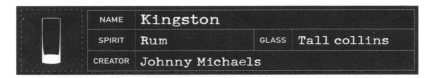

NAME	Kingston		
SPIRIT	Rum	GLASS	Tall collins
CREATOR	Johnny Michaels		

This was another one for Smalley's Caribbean Barbeque and Pirate Bar. It's a collins version of a Hemmingway Daiquiri.

Ingredients

1½ ounces Mount Gay Eclipse gold rum
¾ ounce Luxardo maraschino liqueur
1¼ ounces white grapefruit juice concentrate, defrosted
2 to 3 dashes Allspice Tincture (see p. 196)
3 ounces cold club soda (approximately)
½ or ¼ pink grapefruit wheel (optional)
brandied cherry

Fill a tall collins glass with ice and add all liquid ingredients except club soda. Mix with a straw, top off with club soda, and then just give a poke or two with straw. For some reason, I don't mind mounting the fruit on this one, especially if it's just the ¼ grapefruit wheel. Just place the cherry on the drink's surface—the ice will hold it up.

NAME	Goldfinger		
SPIRIT	Rum	GLASS	Tall collins
CREATOR	Johnny Michaels		

This one is like the first sign of spring light at the end of the cold, dark tunnel of Minnesota winter, or at least the mirage of it. Like a glass of water and a cool tail-wind on mile eighteen of a marathon, this helps keep you going when there are still plenty of miles to go—those hard last miles (not that I'd know). It's a bright, citrusy kalamansi-kumquat mojito that reminds you spring is coming, it will taste like this, and you will smile.

RUM

NORTH STAR COCKTAILS

Ingredients

2 ounces Bacardi Silver rum
1 ounce Minted Kalamansi Sour (see p. 190)
1 ounce Boiron kalamansi purée, defrosted
5 to 6 kumquat halves
lime wedge
10 mint leaves
3 ounces cold club soda (approximately)
orange slice
key lime wheel

In a pint glass, muddle kumquats and lime wedge. Add all liquid ingredients, except club soda, and swirl to free muddled fruit. Pour into tall collins glass with ice. Spank and add mint leaves and top with club soda. Gently mix with a straw. Insert orange slice and lay key lime wheel on drink's surface.

Spanking mint

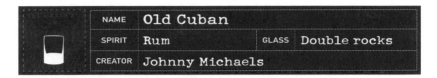

This is La Belle Vie's version of the classic and probably the most popular drink we serve. It's the only drink to be on our list since day one. The main difference is that our version is served on the rocks, whereas the classic is served in a martini glass.

Ingredients

1¾ ounces Mount Gay Eclipse gold rum

¾ ounce Mint Syrup (see p. 182)

2 lime wedges

2 dashes Fee Brothers old-fashioned bitters

5 to 10 fresh mint leaves

2 to 2½ ounces cava (approximately)

In a pint glass, muddle Mint Syrup, bitters, and lime wedges. Add rum and swirl to dislodge muddled fruit. Pour contents into double rocks glass filled with ice and top with cava. Spank mint leaves between palms, add to glass, and mix in with a stir straw.

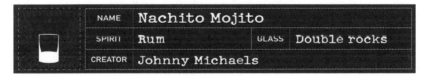

NAME	Nachito Mojito		
SPIRIT	Rum	GLASS	Double rocks
CREATOR	Johnny Michaels		

This one's named after the piano player Nachito Herrera, who was born in Cuba and now lives with his family in White Bear Lake. He and his band play at the Dakota Jazz Club around once a month. I've worked at the Dakota three times, was fired twice (once legitimately), and quit once. I've seen this guy play many times, and when he gets down on the piano, he plays with power! He does Cuba proud (and pisses off the piano tuner on Mondays).

This drink is an Old Cuban with the addition of muddled Fresno pepper. When prepping the pepper, cut off the top and then core out the seeds with a thin, nimble knife. Cut the pepper into slices of equal weight, the wider top slices being

RUM

NORTH STAR COCKTAILS

skinnier than those near the end. (I never use the tail end—you don't want to step on the devil's tail!) It takes a little extra work to pulverize the peppers into pulp, not just crushed big pieces, but as we know, any good bartender has to know how to use a muddler.

Ingredients

1¾ ounces Mount Gay Eclipse gold rum

¾ ounce Mint Syrup (see p. 182)

2 red Fresno pepper slices, seeded

2 lime wedges

2 dashes Fee Brothers old-fashioned bitters

5 to 10 fresh mint leaves

2½ ounces cava (approximately)

In a pint glass, muddle pepper slices with a flat-bottomed wooden muddler. Add Mint Syrup, bitters, and lime wedges and remuddle. Add rum and swirl to dislodge muddled fruit. Pour contents into double rocks glass filled with ice and top with cava. Spank mint leaves between palms, add to glass, and mix in with a stir straw.

	NAME	Le Touriste		
	SPIRIT	Rum	GLASS	Coupe
	CREATOR	Megan Arts		

Ingredients

2½ ounces Martinique *rhum vieux* (aged rum)

¼ ounce Ginger Syrup (see p. 182)

¼ ounce Monin cinnamon syrup

1½ ounces unsweetened coconut milk

dash Angostura bitters

pinch sea salt

lime zest

Shake all ingredients, except zest, with ice and strain into coupe. Using a Microplane grater, grate a small amount of lime zest over surface.

NAME	Mock Wit		
SPIRIT	Rum	GLASS	Collins
CREATOR	Birk Stefan Grudem		

Ingredients

1 ounce Rhum Barbancourt Three Star

1 ounce Cynar

1 ounce fresh grapefruit juice

15 drops Angostura bitters

grapefruit peel coin

Shake all the liquid ingredients with ice and strain into ice-filled collins glass. Squeeze grapefruit coin over drink to express oils and drop in glass.

NAME	Golden Age		
SPIRIT	Rum	GLASS	Rocks
CREATOR	Pip Hanson		

Ingredients

2 ounces Flor de Caña gold rum

1 ounce Tío Pepe fino sherry

1 ounce Cynar

½ ounce Licor 43

3 dashes Peychaud's bitters

grapefruit peel coin

Stir the liquid ingredients with ice and strain into chilled rocks glass. Squeeze grapefruit coin over drink to express oils and drop in glass.

NAME	Privateer		
SPIRIT	Rum	GLASS	Rocks
CREATOR	Pip Hanson		

Ingredients

3 ounces Cruzan Single Barrel rum

1 ounce Punt e Mes vermouth

½ (light) teaspoon Benedictine

dash Angostura bitters

blueberry

Stir all liquid ingredients with ice and strain into chilled rocks glass. Garnish with blueberry.

NAME	Finger Piquin a Six String on Arbol Day		
SPIRIT	Rum	GLASS	Collins
CREATOR	Adam Harness		

This old Town Talk brunch favorite has developed over the years. The name comes from the peppers (pequin and arbol) in Cholula hot sauce.

Ingredients

2 ounces Gosling's rum

½ ounce Cherry Heering

½ orange, juiced

1 teaspoon Cholula hot sauce

grapefruit juice

ginger beer

orange wheel

Shake rum, Cherry Heering, orange juice, and hot sauce with ice. Strain into collins glass with ice and top with equal parts grapefruit juice and ginger beer. Garnish with orange wheel.

NAME	**Hair of the Lion**	
SPIRIT	**Rum**	GLASS **Coupe**
CREATOR	**Adam Harness**	

This riff on the pre-Prohibition Hair of the Lion cocktail replaces whiskey with rum and adds egg white.

Ingredients

2 ounces Appleton Estate Reserve rum

½ ounce St. Elizabeth Allspice Dram

½ ounce simple syrup (see p. 181)

½ ounce fresh lime juice

½ egg white

freshly grated nutmeg

Shake the liquid ingredients vigorously with ice and strain into coupe. Garnish with nutmeg.

Nutmeg and mini grater

Ingredients

1½ ounces Boca Loca cachaça

¾ ounce Green Chartreuse

½ ounce Benedictine

¼ ounce agave nectar

¼ ounce fresh lime juice

brandied cherry

lemon twist

Habanero Tincture (see p. 197)

Shake all the liquid ingredients, except tincture, with ice and strain into cocktail glass. Cut a slit in brandied cherry, wrap around lemon twist, and drop in drink. Add drops of tincture to drink's surface.

NAME	Big Ship		
SPIRIT	Rum	GLASS	Highball
CREATOR	Gina Kent		

Ingredients

1½ ounces Brinley Gold Shipwreck spiced rum

½ ounce Clear Creek pear brandy

¼ ounce St. Elizabeth Allspice Dram

¼ ounce Hazelnut Orgeat (see p. 185)

½ ounce fresh lemon juice

freshly grated nutmeg

Shake the liquid ingredients lightly with ice and strain into ice-filled highball glass. Garnish with nutmeg.

NAME	The Wanderer
SPIRIT	Rum
GLASS	Collins
CREATOR	Nicholas Kosevich and Ira Koplowitz

Ingredients

1¾ ounces Roaring Dan's rum

½ ounce Domaine de Canton ginger liqueur

¼ ounce simple syrup (see p. 181)

¾ ounce fresh lime juice

2 full eyedroppers Bittercube Jamaican #1 bitters

cold club soda

lime wedge

Shake all the liquid ingredients, except soda, with ice and strain into collins glass.
Top with soda and garnish with lime wedge.

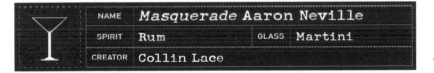

NAME	*Masquerade* Aaron Neville
SPIRIT	Rum
GLASS	Martini
CREATOR	Collin Lace

Ingredients

1½ ounces Chai Tea Rum (see p. 202) lemon wedge

¾ ounce Tuaca liqueur honey

½ ounce Baileys Irish cream ground cardamom

¼ ounce simple syrup (see p. 181) lemon twist

Coat rim of martini glass with honey and then ground cardamom. Squeeze lemon
into an ice-filled shaker and add the liquid ingredients. Shake and pour contents
into martini glass. Garnish with lemon twist.

NAME	Underachiever		
SPIRIT	Rum	GLASS	Collins
CREATOR	Richy Rivera		

Ingredients

1 ounce Bacardi Limón
½ ounce Grand Marnier
½ ounce Arongimon (see below)
2 orange wedges
½ cinnamon, ½ sugar mixture

Rub one orange wedge around rim of collins glass and coat with cinnamon-sugar mixture. Shake the liquid ingredients with ice and strain into ice-filled collins glass. Garnish with remaining orange wedge.

Arongimon

Ingredients

½ cup orange juice concentrate, defrosted
½ cup apple juice concentrate, defrosted
½ cup Monin cinnamon syrup

Mix and store in a 12-ounce squirt bottle.

NAME	Red Stag		
SPIRIT	Rum	GLASS	Pint
CREATOR	Christa Robinson		

This cocktail was made for Kim Bartmann and the Red Stag. In a conversation at the bar one night at Barbette, we both realized that we had based our concepts on the same Wisconsin supper club we had frequented as children.

This one is served at the Red Stag in a large fishbowl glass. At home, a large brandy snifter would work or simply a pint glass.

Ingredients

1 ounce Bacardi Superior rum	½ lime, hollowed out and filled
1 ounce Ketel One vodka	with Jägermeister
½ ounce Cointreau	blood orange wheel
¾ ounce blood orange purée	2 hazelnuts
2 ounces orange juice	

Shake all the liquid ingredients with ice and strain into ice-filled glass. Mount blood orange wheel on rim and float hazelnuts and Jägermeister-filled lime on drink's surface. Serve with a straw.

NAME	Blue Scorpion		
SPIRIT	Rum	GLASS	Tall collins
CREATOR	Sonya Runkle and Geoffrey Trelstad		

This one's in the Don the Beachcomber tradition of delicious and complex fruity cocktails.

Ingredients

2 ounces Mount Gay Eclipse silver rum

½ ounce Velvet Falernum

½ ounce Christian Brothers brandy

½ ounce blue curaçao

1 ounce Lime Sour (see p. 189)

2 ounces orange juice

orange wheel

red maraschino cherry

mint sprig

Shake the liquid ingredients with ice and strain into ice-filled tall collins (aka Zombie) glass. Garnish with orange wheel, cherry, and mint sprig and a parasol and a sipping straw.

NAME	Chupacabra		
SPIRIT	Rum	GLASS	Double rocks
CREATOR	Andy Truskolaski		

Ingredients

2 ounces Velho Barrerio cachaça

2 ounces Bombay Sapphire gin

1 ounce fresh lime juice

1 ounce simple syrup (see p. 181)

½ ounce pineapple juice

1 egg white

1 mango, peeled and cubed

1 serrano pepper slice, seeded

In a Boston shaker, muddle mango and pepper. Add ice and remaining ingredients and shake vigorously. Pour all into double rocks glass.

Brandy

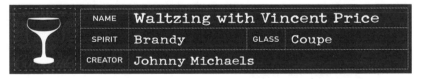

NAME	Bee in the Bonnet		
SPIRIT	Brandy	GLASS	Mini-collins
CREATOR	Johnny Michaels		

This one's a brandy stinger–brandy sour hybrid sweetened with honey, with a touch of heat and a hint of salt. For the garnish, alternately skewer the lemon and orange peel coins, like the stripes on a bee.

Ingredients

2 ounces cognac

1 ounce Clover Honey-Lemon Sour (see p. 191)

2 dashes Hot Pepper Tincture (see p. 195)

2 dashes salt solution (see p. 31)

lemon wedge

2 lemon and 2 orange peel coins, on a 6-inch skewer

Into a cobbler shaker three-quarters full of ice, squeeze and add lemon wedge and then add the liquid ingredients. Shake on medium-high 6 to 8 seconds and then double strain into mini collins glass. Insert skewer with citrus decorations.

NAME	Waltzing with Vincent Price		
SPIRIT	Brandy	GLASS	Coupe
CREATOR	Johnny Michaels		

This drink was inspired by the 1946 black-and-white film *Dragonwyck*, which starred Vincent Price. (Did you know he had his own line of macabre paintings for Sears in the 1960s? The Vincent Price Collection of Fine Art. I wish I had me some of those babies!) If you ever have a dream and you are waltzing with Vincent Price, try to remember to look down at your hand. I'm sure you will see an etched-crystal coupe glass, and it will have this cocktail in it. Don't worry. It won't spill. Just let yourself go and give in to the magic of the waltz. Did I just say that? #%*! me.

Ingredients

2 ounces calvados or cognac

¼ ounce 20-year tawny port

¼ ounce Benedictine

2 dashes Angostura bitters

1 to 2 ounces dry French cider

3 or 4 thin apple slices

Gently swirl all liquids except the cider in a Boston tin with minimal ice. Strain into chilled coupe and top with cider (you could substitute any sparkling cider, but Vincent would prefer you open a bottle of expensive French cider, even if just to use an ounce. You could always pour some out for the homies). Garnish with a fan of thin apple slices on drink's surface.

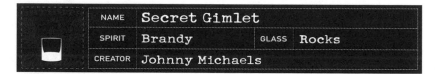

	NAME	Secret Gimlet		
	SPIRIT	Brandy	GLASS	Rocks
	CREATOR	Johnny Michaels		

People go for the mysterious names, and I really dug this one. I like using white brandy, sort of like vodka with more body. (Come to find out a lot of liquor companies add caramel color to their spirits to enhance the aged look, pumping the liquid in one side of a barrel and out the other—tadah, it's been barrel aged.) In the original menu description, I think I wrote, "Only Johnny knows and he isn't telling/can't remember," so people wouldn't hassle the cocktail servers too much about what was in it. Then, sure enough, I had a hell of a time remembering the recipe for this book (which, since I haven't kept a list of cocktail names or recipes since La Belle Vie opened in Minneapolis in 2005, was pretty much the same hard rock mining all the way through).

Ingredients

1 ounce Christian Brothers Frost White brandy

1 ounce Gordon's gin

½ ounce Lime Sour (see p. 189)

½ ounce Fire Woman Mix (see p. 40)

½ ounce Aperol   blood orange slice

lime wedge   key lime wheel

Into a pint glass 60 percent full of ice, squeeze and add lime and then add the liquid ingredients. Cap and shake vigorously 6 seconds and then pour contents into rocks glass. Garnish by laying blood orange slice on drink's surface and key lime wheel on top of that, lining up center points of the wheels so that a subtle eye is hidden in there.

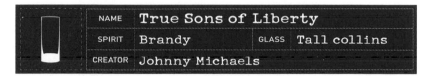

	NAME	True Sons of Liberty		
	SPIRIT	Brandy	GLASS	Tall collins
	CREATOR	Johnny Michaels		

When the 2008 Republican National Convention was coming to the Twin Cities, we thought we were going to get crushed, being a fancy restaurant and all. (We escaped with a slow week. Apparently, we don't serve enough steak or were blackballed for having too many liberal employees.) So I came up with a couple drink names that I thought suited middle-aged men would hit on, Home of the Brave being another. Anyway, I liked True Sons of Liberty because it was the name of a hardcore punk band that came out of California in the late seventies. I envisioned these guys guffawing and saying how much they liked the True Sons of Liberty. It was going to be my mental Gatorade, and then the storm never came—no complaints, here.

Ingredients

2 ounces Laird's 80-proof applejack

2 ounces Apple-Ginger-Lemon Sour (see p. 190)

2½ ounces cava (approximately)

5 Honeycrisp apple slices

To a tall collins glass with ice, add applejack and sour. Mix with a straw, add a couple more ice cubes, and top with cava. Garnish with apple slices mounted on the rim, pointing upward and outward. (What was I thinking? What Republican would drink something that looked like that? Plenty of people seem to like it, though.)

innesota Historical Society Press
#3694 Michael / Northstar Cocktails
book 1p — 9/6/11 — pg 125
Phoenix Type, Inc.

	NAME	Bunyan, Clyde Bunyan		
	SPIRIT	Brandy	GLASS	Rocks
	CREATOR	Johnny Michaels		

This is a tough, tough, tough drink. It's surprising the difference the liquors' being 10 percent stronger makes. Nobody ever finishes it without taking a knee at one point. It's a total winter cocktail. I infuse my maple syrup with crushed red pepper at La Belle Vie, but this is the home version.

Ingredients

1¼ ounces Laird's 100-proof applejack
1¼ ounces Wild Turkey 101-proof rye
½ ounce Grade B maple syrup
2 dashes Hot Pepper Tincture (see p. 195)
dash Angostura bitters
1 or 3 apple slices

Add liquid ingredients to rocks glass and mix. Top with ice and insert apple slice(s). Good luck.

	NAME	On the Night He Was Betrayed		
	SPIRIT	Brandy	GLASS	Rocks
	CREATOR	Johnny Michaels		

Here's another dark-side holiday drink, this one for Easter. The name is a line from Catholic Mass. I'm kind of always dialed in to be thinking of good drink names. Sometimes someone says something, and I'll be, like, *Drink Name*—I'm using that. This one hit me at my father's funeral mass. Amari are very fashionable nowadays, Fernet-Branca in particular. I've seen a lot of recipes where the Fernet-Branca looked like it was forced, staple-gunned onto a cocktail. I like this one, though. It really fits the theme of this drink, and I just dig the Fernet-Branca, blackberry, and lemon combo. This drink works great with whiskey, too.

Ingredients

1½ ounces cognac or brandy   ½ ounce Lemon Sour (see p. 189)

½ ounce Monin blackberry syrup   lemon wedge

½ ounce Fernet-Branca   lemon wheel

Into a pint glass two-thirds full of ice, squeeze and discard lemon wedge and then add the liquid ingredients. Cap and shake on medium 5 seconds or so. Pour contents into rocks glass and insert lemon wheel.

NAME	The Angel's Share		
SPIRIT	Brandy	GLASS	Tall collins
CREATOR	Johnny Michaels		

This drink was inspired by a Banksy graffiti piece. In an abandoned, boarded-up, and dilapidated doorway somewhere in New Orleans, there's this white-painted stencil of an angel, with wings and a halo, sitting against the wall, slumped over and smoking a cigarette, with a bottle of booze by his feet. At first I was going to call this one Just Taking a Break, but it didn't ring true. At any rate, I remembered hearing about kids in Spain drinking red wine and Coke and Argentineans drinking Fernet-Branca and Coke and decided to go with it. To serve, I photocopied that picture out of a Banksy book, and we use them as bev naps for the drink. Since it was a picture of public graffiti, I figured he wouldn't mind. It's not like we're getting rich off it, and if you didn't know who Banksy is, well, now you do.

Ingredients

1½ ounces brandy or cognac

½ ounce Fernet-Branca

¾ ounce fresh Lemon Sweet and Sour

½ ounce big red wine (cabernet sauvignon, Super Tuscan, whatever)

2 ounces cola

lemon wheel

innesota Historical Society Press
#3694 Michael / *Northstar Cocktails*
book 1p — 9/6/11 — pg 127
Phoenix Type, Inc.

To a tall collins glass full of ice, add all the liquid ingredients except cola and mix with a straw. Top off glass with ice and then cola. Insert lemon wheel. Place cocktail in the open spot above the fallen angel and between the pillars on the bev nap.

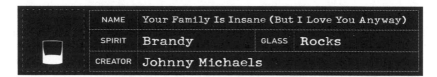

	NAME	Your Family Is Insane (But I Love You Anyway)
	SPIRIT	**Brandy** GLASS **Rocks**
	CREATOR	**Johnny Michaels**

One of the more popular cocktails from The 12 Drinks of Christmas we did in 2009, which almost killed me (way too much work). I've worried someone might read the drink name, laugh a little too enthusiastically for their partner's taste, and end up on the couch for a night or two. I've also liked to think that on Christmas day somewhere, somebody might be sitting at a dinner table, listening to some unbelievable conversation, remembering this drink's name, and just smiling politely while they take it all in. It's funny how this drink sells more the week after Christmas than it does the week before it.

Ingredients

2 ounces Sugar Plum Brandy (see p. 200)
2 to 3 orange slices
½ ounce Demerara Syrup (see p. 181)
2 dashes Christmas Bitters (see below)
brandied cherry, on a 6-inch skewer

In an empty rocks glass, muddle orange slices with syrup and Christmas Bitters. You want to crush the juices and oils out, not pulverize the fruit and get a bunch of pulp floating around the drink. Add brandy and swirl around a bit to blend. Top with ice and insert cherry skewer. Try not to laugh at the name again—think of your poor back—unless you have a real comfortable couch.

Christmas Bitters

I'm pretty sure these spices are used in the production of Angostura bitters. Their recipe is a secret, so we are just adjusting the EQ to boost the Christmas flavors. It's a lot easier than making a batch from scratch, and the quality is probably better than what a person can make at home. Angostura is pretty much considered the king of bitters (although the Bitter Truth has come out with a variety that some say is as good, maybe better).

I use crushed pieces because powders can be really difficult to strain out, unless you buy an expensive Büchner funnel from a chemistry supply store, and I've always had trouble with mine.

Ingredients

4 ounces Angostura bitters

1 tablespoon crushed nutmeg

1 tablespoon smashed dried ginger pieces

2 teaspoons whole cloves

Toast cloves lightly over medium-low heat in a metal-clad skillet, to bloom the spice. Add all ingredients to a mason jar and let sit 1 week, shaking daily. Strain through a cheesecloth-lined fine-mesh strainer and funnel into an eyedropper bottle.

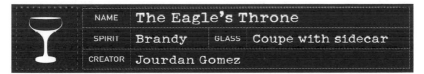

NAME	The Eagle's Throne		
SPIRIT	Brandy	GLASS	Coupe with sidecar
CREATOR	Jourdan Gomez		

Ingredients

1 ounce Laird's applejack

1 (light) ounce Cynar

¾ ounce Punt e Mes vermouth

½ ounce Don Julio añejo tequila

¼ ounce Amaro Nonino

dash orange bitters

Sombra mezcal

grapefruit peel coin

Rinse coupe with mezcal, discarding excess. Fill mixing glass with ice and pour in remaining liquids. Stir and strain into coupe and sidecar. Pinch grapefruit coin over cocktail to express oils and discard.

innesota Historical Society Press
#3694 Michael / *Northstar Cocktails*
book 1p — 9/6/11 — pg 129
Phoenix Type, Inc.

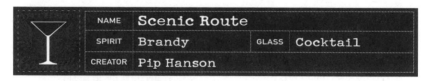

Make the simple syrup at a ratio of 2 parts sugar to 1 part water.

Ingredients

2½ ounces Ginger Applejack (see p. 200)

1 ounce fresh lemon juice

¼ (light) ounce simple syrup

¼ (light) ounce Cointreau

dash Disaronno amaretto

lemon wedge

Spiced Sugar (see below)

Rub rim of chilled cocktail glass with lemon wedge and coat with Spiced Sugar. Shake all the liquid ingredients with ice and strain into glass.

Spiced Sugar

Ingredients

5 tablespoons sugar

1 tablespoon ground cinnamon

1 tablespoon freshly ground nutmeg

1 tablespoon ground cayenne

Mix and store in a sealed container.

NAME	Pinkerton
SPIRIT	Brandy
GLASS	Rocks
CREATOR	Rob Jones

This cocktail is based on an old Jerry Thomas recipe, the Japanese Cocktail.

Ingredients

1 ounce good (not expensive) cognac
1 ounce overproof rye
¼ (heavy) ounce orgeat
3 big dashes Angostura bitters
orange peel coin

Stir all the liquid ingredients in a pint glass with ice and strain into ice-filled rocks glass. Squeeze orange peel over cocktail to express oils and then drop into drink.

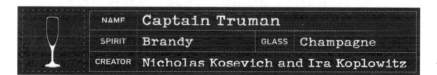

NAME	Captain Truman
SPIRIT	Brandy
GLASS	Champagne
CREATOR	Nicholas Kosevich and Ira Koplowitz

Ingredients

1 ounce Paul Masson brandy
¾ ounce Domaine de Canton ginger liqueur
¾ ounce fresh lemon juice
½ ounce simple syrup (see p. 181)
15 drops Bittercube Bolivar bitters
1½ ounces sparkling wine
lemon twist

Shake all the liquid ingredients, except champagne, with ice and strain into champagne flute. Top with sparkling wine and garnish with lemon twist.

innesota Historical Society Press
#3694 Michael / *Northstar Cocktails*
book 1p — 9/6/11 — pg 131
Phoenix Type, Inc.

NAME	La Pâquerette		
SPIRIT	Brandy	GLASS	Rocks
CREATOR	Nicholas Kosevich and Ira Koplowitz		

Ingredients

1 ounce Tariquet armagnac

½ ounce fresh lemon juice

¼ ounce Grand Marnier

¼ ounce simple syrup (see p. 181)

15 drops Bittercube cherry bark–vanilla bitters

cold club soda

Shake all the liquid ingredients, except club soda, with ice and strain into ice-filled rocks glass. Top with club soda.

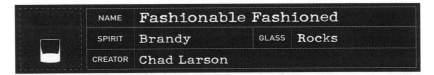

NAME	Fashionable Fashioned		
SPIRIT	Brandy	GLASS	Rocks
CREATOR	Chad Larson		

Ingredients

2 ounces Laird's applejack

¼ ounce simple syrup (see p. 181)

dash Cinnamon Tincture (see p. 196)

orange peel coin

4 drops Bittercube cherry bark–vanilla bitters

brandied cherry

Muddle orange peel, syrup, and bitters gently in the bottom of rocks glass. Add applejack and tincture and stir. Add ice (a single large cube if you can) and stir to slightly chill. Garnish with brandied cherry.

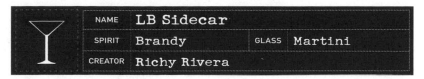

NAME	LB Sidecar		
SPIRIT	Brandy	GLASS	Martini
CREATOR	Richy Rivera		

Ingredients

- 1½ ounces cognac
- 1 ounce Cointreau
- 1 ounce Lemon-Basil Syrup (see p. 187)
- 2 lemon wedges
- Basil Sugar (see below)

Rub one of the lemon wedges around the rim of martini glass and coat with Basil Sugar. Shake the liquid ingredients with ice and strain into martini glass. Garnish with remaining lemon wedge.

Basil Sugar

Ingredients

- 2 cups sugar
- ½ ounce fresh basil

Mix in a food processor. Sift sugar mixture in a sifter or in a bowl with a whisk. Store in an airtight container.

BRANDY

133

NORTH STAR COCKTAILS

innesota Historical Society Press
#3694 Michael / *Northstar Cocktails*
book 1p — 9/6/11 — pg 133
Phoenix Type, Inc.

Whiskey

NAME	Grinch Nog		
SPIRIT	Whiskey	GLASS	Martini
CREATOR	Johnny Michaels		

Here's a favorite for people a bit jaded about Christmas, or just sick of all the cutesy holiday specials, and one of my first whiskey-gin combos, which is an idea I really dig. People often ask, How can this drink be called a nog if it contains no egg? I explain that I called the Grinch (I've got his cell number, you know, birds of a feather) and asked him as politely as I could. There was a long, silent pause, and then he told me to #%*! off and hung up.

Ingredients

1½ ounces Wild Turkey 101-proof or Rittenhouse 100-proof rye

1½ ounces Beefeater gin

½ ounce maraschino liqueur

¼ ounce absinthe

½ ounce Lemon Sour (see p. 189)

2 dashes Fee Brothers old-fashioned bitters

dash Angostura bitters

dash Regan's or Angostura orange bitters

1 or 2 dashes salt solution (see p. 31)

lemon wedge

green maraschino cherry, on a 6-inch skewer

Into a Boston tin half full of ice, squeeze and add lemon wedge and then add the liquid ingredients. Swirl until proper (this one takes a lot of swirling) and strain into martini glass. Garnish with skewer across top of glass.

Grinch Nog

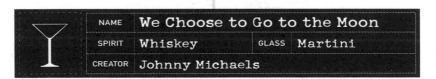

NAME	We Choose to Go to the Moon		
SPIRIT	Whiskey	GLASS	Martini
CREATOR	Johnny Michaels		

This one was very popular, a top-ten drink, but a lot of work to prep, make, and carbonate. It had perfect synergy between name and cocktail when it came out in 2009, the fortieth-anniversary year of the moon landing. We won that space race! This drink needs to be made in big batches, chilled, bottled, and then carbonated.

Ingredients

8 ounces Rittenhouse 100-proof rye

8 ounces Cabin Still 80-proof bourbon

2 ounces maraschino dry cherry brandy

3 ounces Noilly Prat sweet vermouth

8 ounces Coke Syrup (see p. 185)

2 ounces Adriatic or Marco Polo sour cherry syrup or Monin cherry syrup

½ ounce Fee Brothers original bitters

½ ounce Angostura bitters

Mix all ingredients and funnel into a 1-liter bottle. Chill and then carbonate according to manufacturer's instructions. (You want to chill the liquid before you carbonate it. For some reason it holds more gas that way.) To serve, very slowly (to preserve
carbonation) pour 5 ounces into a Boston tin 80 percent full of ice. Let it sit for a
bit and still chill and then strain into martini glass. Garnish with a skewered brandy
cherry across top of glass.

	NAME	The Future Ghost		
	SPIRIT	Whiskey	GLASS	Bordeaux
	CREATOR	Johnny Michaels		

It pains me to say this, but I can't tell you the name of the man who inspired this
cocktail, and I can't say why. He's a jazz musician. He's half in this world, half in his
own. He is one cool cat, one of the only guys who makes me want to go out and buy
a suit. He's a deep-sea diver. You've got to be if you can string pearls like this guy. I
wanted you to know his name, so if you hadn't heard his music, you could go check
it out if you knew what was good for you. I think if roles were reversed, I wouldn't be
mad, maybe a bit disconcerted, just as disconcerted as I was the minute I realized it
might take one to know one. So if you really want to know, ask around. Maybe that's
how it should be, by word of mouth. That's how you get in, you know. The doorman
smells your breath, and he can tell. Last thing I'll say, *The Future Ghost* would make a
great album title if you knew you had found a pile of golden acorns rolling around,
slow-motion style, on the pitch-black ocean floor.

This one's a Sazerac-Manhattan hybrid, served in a bordeaux wineglass. Bourbon
drinks sometimes taste better when they're a little warmer, and chilling can emas-
culate whiskey, so this one gets chilled, but not too much. Also, when spraying the
inside of the wineglass, make sure not to be too close, where you'll mainly hit the
bottom of the glass, or too far away, where you'll hit the outside of the glass. You
want it to be right in the middle, where it mists the inside of the glass pretty evenly.
And use a small, breath spray–sized bottle, because a bigger one will deliver too
much absinthe.

Ingredients

3 ounces Jim Beam Black bourbon
½ ounce Devil Mix (see p. 140)
½ ounce Noilly Prat sweet vermouth
½ ounce big red wine (cabernet sauvignon, Super Tuscan, whatever)
1 spray Pine Smoke Absinthe (see p. 198)

Spray inside of bordeaux wineglass with Pine Smoke Absinthe. To a Boston tin with maybe 1 to 1½ inches of ice, add remaining ingredients and lightly swirl-chill a bit and then strain into glass, right into the bottom. You don't want to wash the inside walls of the glass clean.

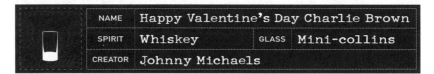

NAME	Happy Valentine's Day Charlie Brown		
SPIRIT	Whiskey	GLASS	Mini-collins
CREATOR	Johnny Michaels		

I like making up jaded holiday drink names; they totally cheer up cynical people. Everyone's serving smiley, happy, holiday drinks—including us—but we take care of the jaded people who possess a good sense of humor, too (plus they tend to be good drinkers). The drink is garnished with a plain wooden skewer with a barb near the tip. When people ask about the barb, I explain that sometimes Cupid's Arrow turns into the Chump Harpoon.

Ingredients

4 ounces Rittenhouse 100-proof rye
½ ounce Luxardo maraschino liqueur
2 dashes Cinnamon Tincture (see p. 196)
dash Angostura bitters
6-inch skewer, with ¾ inch snapped off blunt end and a
      barbed tip (see instructions)

To a Boston tin half full of ice, add liquid ingredients and swirl until proper. Strain into mini-collins glass. Make the barb on the skewer with a small, thin, sharp knife. Please be careful.

NAME	**Knife in the Water**	
SPIRIT	Whiskey	GLASS Rocks
CREATOR	Johnny Michaels	

This drink's name, from the Polanski film, was the longest-lived resident in my drink name orphanage. It was there for over five years without a home. I never felt anything was quite the right match. Then, this past winter, I made a new-school old-fashioned with blood orange, rye, and gin. The gin cut the rye, and the name finally had a drink.

Ingredients

1½ ounces Wild Turkey 101-proof rye

1½ ounces Bombay Sapphire gin

3 blood orange slices

½ ounce Demerara Syrup (see p. 181)

2 dashes Angostura or Regan's orange bitters

2 dashes Angostura bitters

brandied cherry, on a 6-inch skewer

In rocks glass, muddle blood orange wheels, bitters, and syrup with a flat-bottomed wooden muddler. Crush but do not pulverize fruit. Add rye and gin, swirl to combine flavors, and top with ice. Garnish with skewered cherry.

NAME	**Handsome Devil**	
SPIRIT	Whiskey	GLASS Rocks
CREATOR	Johnny Michaels	

Every now and then, you get lucky, and for this one, I thank the Powers That Be. Also, another one named after a Smiths' song.

Ingredients

2 ounces Jim Beam Black bourbon
½ (heavy) ounce Devil Mix (see below)
orange slice
brandied cherry, on a 6-inch skewer
blanched hazelnut

Add bourbon and Devil Mix to rocks glass and then add ice. Insert orange slice like a mohawk, so that the top of the peel is sticking out. Insert skewered cherry and drop hazelnut in drink.

Devil Mix

Ingredients

4 ounces Benedictine
4 ounces Frangelico
4 ounces Cointreau
½ ounce salt solution (see p. 31)
½ ounce Hot Pepper Tincture (see p. 195)
¼ ounce Angostura bitters
¼ ounce Regan's orange bitters
¼ ounce Fee Brothers old-fashioned bitters

Mix and store in a bottle. Makes enough for about 20 cocktails.

	NAME	Molly McNasty		
	SPIRIT	Whiskey	GLASS	Double rocks
	CREATOR	Johnny Michaels		

This one was our first St. Patrick's Day drink (it's so nice to work in a bar that doesn't get crushed on St. Patrick's Day). It's a very nice spring drink, named after one of our sweet La Belle Vie lounge cocktailers, Molly "McSwiggin" Sullivan, who is very proud of her Irish heritage and not at all nasty. I love using Green Chartreuse, especially in the spring and summer.

Ingredients

1¾ ounces Jameson Irish whiskey

¾ ounce Green Chartreuse

¾ ounce Lemon Sour (see p. 189)

¼ ounce Mint Syrup (see p. 182)

½ ounce cold club soda

lemon wheel, with a mint leaf plastered to it

To a pint glass 90 percent full of ice, add all the liquid ingredients except club soda. Cap and give a good shaking to it for about 5 seconds. Pour a splash of club soda in double rocks glass and then pour contents of shaker on top. Garnish by laying the pretty lemon wheel with the mint leaf on top of the drink's surface.

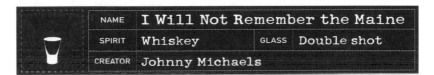

	NAME	I Will Not Remember the Maine		
	SPIRIT	Whiskey	GLASS	Double shot
	CREATOR	Johnny Michaels		

Remember the Maine is a classic, though semi-obscure, cocktail. Though I mean no disrespect to any of the lost souls from the sinking of the *Maine*—and I acknowledge that classic cocktails are awesome—I just refuse to believe that there are no more great undiscovered cocktails (see Pip Hanson's Oliveto for proof), so this name is a subtle dig at the crowd who believes that everything's been done already. I dig this drink. It was inspired by the classic one but actually bears very little resemblance to it. (I have also nicknamed it "To Die by the Sword" because the process of trying to remember all these cocktail recipes I had never written down has resulted in me sipping on a few of these while staring at the computer and my multi-measurement clear shot glass jigger.)

Ingredients

¾ ounce rye

¾ ounce gin

¼ ounce maraschino liqueur

1 (heavy) dash Angostura bitters

Pour liquids into double shot glass and insert a large ice cube.

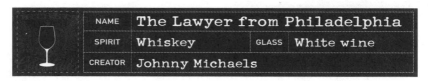

NAME	The Lawyer from Philadelphia		
SPIRIT	Whiskey	GLASS	White wine
CREATOR	Johnny Michaels		

This one gets its name from a tirade somebody posted on eGullet using old-timey slang, ripping on anyone who didn't make true Old-Fashioneds (whiskey, sugar, bitters). The poster wrote that he didn't want "some lawyer from Philadelphia" putting fruit in his Old-Fashioned. It inspired me to make this pink, bourbon-based cocktail, which is served in a white wine glass and garnished with a pansy rested atop a floating lemon wheel. A very nice and summery bourbon cocktail.

Ingredients

2 ounces Cabin Still bourbon
¾ ounce Aperol
½ ounce Lemon Sour (see p. 189)
lemon wedge

dash Fee Brothers rhubarb
bitters
lemon wheel
pansy flower

Into a Boston shaker half full of ice, squeeze and add lemon wedge and then add liquid ingredients. Cap and shake 3 to 4 seconds. Strain into a white wine glass and add a few fresh chips or cracked cubes of ice. Place lemon wheel flat on cocktail's surface and place flower on top of lemon wheel.

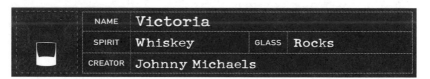

NAME	Victoria		
SPIRIT	Whiskey	GLASS	Rocks
CREATOR	Johnny Michaels		

This is an old drink, one of the originals from our opening list at La Belle Vie in 2005. It seems so outdated now, but still simple and good. I originally used Crown Royal, but any Canadian whiskey works fine. American blended whiskey or bourbon would also work well if you hate Canadians for some reason.

Ingredients

2½ ounces Canadian whiskey

⅓ ounce Grade B maple syrup

dash Angostura bitters

dash Fee Brothers old-fashioned bitters

Pour everything into an empty rocks glass, stir to blend, and top with ice.

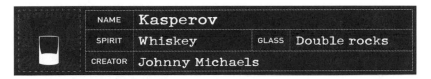

	NAME	Kasperov		
	SPIRIT	Whiskey	GLASS	Double rocks
	CREATOR	Johnny Michaels		

Also known as Eye of the Tiger, this is a great late-winter, early-spring cocktail. It was created to kick the ass of Jameson ginger ales.

Ingredients

2 ounces Canadian Mist or other light-bodied whiskey

½ ounce orange juice concentrate, defrosted

½ ounce Ginger Syrup (see p. 182)

2 dashes Cinnamon Tincture (see p. 196)

1 dash orange bitters

2 ounces cava (approximately)

orange slice

1 piece candied ginger, on a 6-inch skewer

To an ice-filled double rocks glass, add all liquid ingredients except cava and stir. Top with cava and give another poke or two to mix. Insert orange slice and candied ginger skewer.

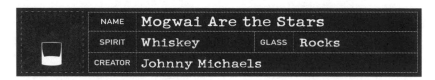

NAME	Mogwai Are the Stars		
SPIRIT	Whiskey	GLASS	Rocks
CREATOR	Johnny Michaels		

Mogwai is a band from Scotland, and they are my favorite. I made up this scotch cocktail in their honor before they played First Avenue in 2009. I sent a letter through their manager encouraging the band to stop by La Belle Vie after sound check and try it out, even though I figured they—being Scottish and all—would probably kick my ass for putting anything into scotch. I like the sweet-salty-savory taste with a heat finish—a nice, sustaining feedback, just like Mogwai does it (when they want to).

Ingredients

2 ounces Dewar's blended scotch

1 soup spoon Habanero-Butterscotch Syrup (see p. 183)

dash Laphroaig single-malt scotch

To a rocks glass, add Dewar's and syrup, stirring with spoon to blend. Fill glass with ice and then drizzle a little Laphroaig on top. Do not stir or garnish with a stir straw. You want the peaty nose of the single malt on top and the smooth blended scotch in the body.

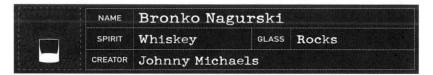

NAME	Bronko Nagurski		
SPIRIT	Whiskey	GLASS	Rocks
CREATOR	Johnny Michaels		

This drink has good synergy. Bronko was from the Iron Range and played football for the Gophers. The drink's made with rye, which was the preferred whiskey of America back in the day, and root beer is an old-time flavor too. This one is so simple, but it's such a crowd pleaser.

Ingredients

2 ounces Rittenhouse 100-proof rye

¼ ounce Torani root beer syrup

dash Angostura bitters

dash Fee Brothers old-fashioned bitters

dash Regan's orange bitters

Pour ingredients into rocks glass and stir with a spoon. Add ice and serve.

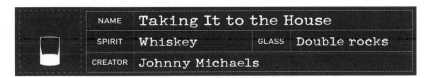

	NAME	Taking It to the House		
	SPIRIT	Whiskey	GLASS	Double rocks
	CREATOR	Johnny Michaels		

Here's a great fall drink. I was originally going to call this one Flavor Country but renamed it to make one of our top FoodCookers happy when he was having a tough week. It's his phrase for when he drinks over half a bottle of Crown Royal and does himself proper, and yes, he's from the South.

Ingredients

2 ounces bourbon (I like Jim Beam Black in this one)

½ ounce Benedictine

1½ ounces Apple-Ginger-Lemon Sour (see p. 190)

3 strong dashes Angostura bitters

3 red apple slices (preferably Honeycrisp)

To a pint glass filled with ice, add all liquid ingredients. Cap with tin and power-shake 6 to 7 seconds. Pour contents into double rocks glass and garnish by fanning apple slices like an airplane propeller.

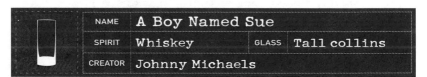

	NAME	Don't Mind If I Do		
	SPIRIT	Whiskey	GLASS	Double rocks
	CREATOR	Johnny Michaels		

This is a summer favorite. I refuse to make it until the black cherries are prime, ripe and inexpensive. This is another drink name people like to say, like to order: they get a kick out of it. There's been more than one "Who's On First" moment between server and guest with this one.

Ingredients

2 ounces bourbon (Cabin Still for value or Jim Beam Black
    for flavor)
2 ounces Cherry-Lemon Sour (see p. 190)
lemon wheel
2 fresh black cherries, pitted, on a 6-inch skewer

To a pint glass full of ice, add bourbon and sour. Cap with tin and powershake vigorously 5 to 10 seconds. Pour contents into double rocks glass and garnish by partially submerging the lemon wheel in the drink (do not mount on rim, please) and inserting wooden skewer so that the cherries are at the drink's surface.

	NAME	A Boy Named Sue		
	SPIRIT	Whiskey	GLASS	Tall collins
	CREATOR	Johnny Michaels		

I have been nicknamed "Johnny Cash" by at least three different Hispanic dishwashers at different restaurants over the years. I've always thought it was funny and took it as a true compliment. I wear all black a lot of the time, and we have some other similarities. I like to say that Johnny Cash has always struck me as the kind of guy who ate only one piece of fruit a year, and with a name like *nectarine,* that was what he probably picked most of the time. I just can't see him eating a banana. I could see him waxing poetically, spoken-word style, about the nectarine while softly strumming his guitar for about half an hour before eating it—and then he would throw it up. People are always appalled by that surprise ending. I thought and still think it's hilarious, but I've walked in those moccasins, so I figure I'm allowed to laugh. I mean no disrespect: I am a big fan.

Ingredients

2 ounces Jim Beam bourbon

1½ ounces Ginger-Lemon Sour
    (see p. 190)

2 dashes Johnny Cash Bitters
    (see below)

1½ ounces cava

beef jerky stick

lemon wheel

2 nectarine slices

pansy flower

To an ice-filled tall collins glass, add bourbon, syrup, and bitters and poke with a straw or chopstick to stir. Top with cava (no more than 1½ ounces). Insert beef jerky, lemon wheel, and nectarine slices and top with pansy. How do you do, indeed.

Johnny Cash Bitters

Ingredients

2 ounces Tobacco Tincture (see p. 196)

1 ounce Angostura bitters

1 ounce Fee Brothers peach bitters

Mix and store in an eyedropper bottle or empty bitters bottle. Note: the tincture contains nicotine. You can substitute an additional ounce of Angostura bitters instead.

NAME	Broken Halo		
SPIRIT	Whiskey	GLASS	Coupe
CREATOR	Megan Arts		

Ingredients

1½ ounces rye

1½ ounces Amaro Averna

½ ounce simple syrup (see p. 181)

1 ounce fresh Meyer lemon juice

1 egg white

pinch cayenne

3 dashes mole bitters

lemon peel spiral

Shake cayenne and all liquid ingredients except bitters and strain into coupe. Dash bitters over the froth and garnish with lemon spiral.

NAME	Frontier Law		
SPIRIT	Whiskey	GLASS	Rocks with sidecar
CREATOR	Birk Stefan Grudem		

Ingredients

2 ounces Old Weller 107-proof bourbon

½ ounce Drambuie

¾ ounce Carpano Antica sweet vermouth

13 drops Bittercube Bolivar bitters

Flamed Absinthe with Rosewater spritz (see below)

Stir bourbon, Drambuie, vermouth, and bitters with ice. Strain low into ice-filled rock glass and pour remainder into sidecar. Hold a lit lighter between glass and atomizer and spray so that flamed mist coats inside of glass.

Flamed Absinthe with Rosewater

Ingredients

¾ ounce Pernod absinthe   ¼ ounce rosewater

Mix and store in an atomizer or small spray bottle.

NAME	Bitter Branch		
SPIRIT	Whiskey	GLASS	Rocks
CREATOR	Pip Hanson		

Make the salt solution at a ratio of 1 part kosher salt to 3 parts hot water.

Ingredients

3 ounces Rittenhouse rye	dash (about 12 drops) salt
1 ounce Cynar	solution
½ ounce Nocello walnut liqueur	candied walnut

Stir liquid ingredients with ice and strain into chilled rocks glass. Garnish with candied walnut.

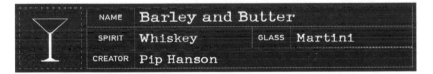

NAME	Blood on the Rocks		
SPIRIT	Whiskey	GLASS	Highball
CREATOR	Pip Hanson		

Make the simple syrup at a ratio of 2 parts sugar to 1 part water.

Ingredients

2½ ounces Jim Beam Black bourbon

1 ounce fresh lemon juice

¾ ounce simple syrup

dash Tabasco

1 ounce red wine (approximately)

Shake all ingredients except red wine with ice and strain into highball full of ice. Top with red wine. Do not stir.

NAME	Barley and Butter		
SPIRIT	Whiskey	GLASS	Martini
CREATOR	Pip Hanson		

Make the honey syrup by dissolving 2 parts honey in 1 part boiling water.

Ingredients

3 ounces Butter-Washed Scotch (see p. 201)

1 ounce Johnny Walker Red blended scotch

¼ ounce oloroso sherry

¼ ounce honey syrup

4 dashes Peychaud's bitters

orange peel coin

Stir all liquid ingredients with ice and strain into chilled martini glass. Squeeze orange coin over drink and drop in.

NAME	Redcoat		
SPIRIT	Whiskey	GLASS	Rocks
CREATOR	Pip Hanson		

Ingredients

1½ ounces Rittenhouse 100-proof rye

1½ ounces Campari

dash Regan's orange bitters

2¼ ounces Bell's Two Hearted ale (approximately)

Place a large piece of ice in a chilled rocks glass. Build drink over ice in order given and stir gently.

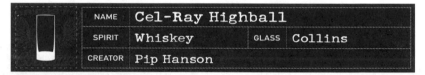

NAME	Cel-Ray Highball		
SPIRIT	Whiskey	GLASS	Collins
CREATOR	Pip Hanson		

Ingredients

dash Peychaud's bitters

2 ounces Dewar's blended scotch

Dr. Brown's Cel-Ray Soda

celery stick

cherry tomato

In a collins glass filled with ice, build ingredients in order given and top with soda. Garnish with celery stick and cherry tomato.

NAME	Fernet Julep		
SPIRIT	Whiskey	GLASS	Coupe
CREATOR	Pip Hanson		

Juleps are traditionally served in silver or pewter cups. A cobbler shaker's tin can work as a substitute.

*Pip Hanson displays proper pinkie
flaring technique*

Ingredients

1¼ ounces Knob Creek bourbon   dash Demerara Syrup (see p. 181)

1½ ounces Fernet-Branca   1 mint sprig tip

21 mint leaves

In a cobbler tin, gently bruise mint leaves into Fernet-Branca and add bourbon and syrup. Fill with crushed ice and garnish with mint sprig. Serve with a thick straw cut short so that it barely protrudes past sprig.

NAME	Angophile		
SPIRIT	Whiskey	GLASS	Rocks
CREATOR	Pip Hanson		

Ingredients

1 ounce Knob Creek bourbon   ¾ ounce Licor 43

1 ounce Angostura bitters   1 egg

Shake all ingredients hard without ice 20 seconds. Add ice and shake hard again. Strain into short tumbler or chilled rocks glass.

NAME	Copper Creel		
SPIRIT	Whiskey	GLASS	Coupe
CREATOR	Jesse Held		

Ingredients

1½ ounces single-malt scotch (I use Drumguish)

¾ ounce Carpano Antica sweet vermouth

½ ounce Royal Combier orange liqueur

½ ounce Drambuie

lemon peel spiral

Stir liquid ingredients with ice and strain into coupe. Garnish with lemon spiral.

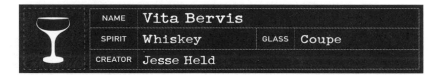

NAME	Vita Bervis		
SPIRIT	Whiskey	GLASS	Coupe
CREATOR	Jesse Held		

Ingredients

2 ounces Old Overholt rye

¾ ounce Cocchi Aperitivo Americano

¾ ounce Aperol

absinthe spritz, from an atomizer

Stir all except absinthe with ice and strain into coupe. Spritz absinthe over top of drink.

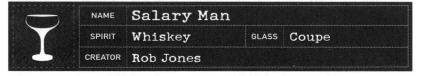

NAME	Salary Man		
SPIRIT	Whiskey	GLASS	Coupe
CREATOR	Rob Jones		

Ingredients

2 ounces Famous Grouse scotch

1 ounce Carpano Antica sweet vermouth

½ ounce Amaro Nonino

9 drops Bittercube cherry bark–vanilla bitters

absinthe

Rinse coupe with absinthe, discarding excess. Fill mixing glass with ice and pour in scotch, vermouth, and Amaro Nonino. Stir and strain into coupe. Top with bitters.

	NAME	Breakfast in Vermont		
	SPIRIT	Whiskey	GLASS	Rocks
	CREATOR	Shawn Jones		

Ingredients

2 ounces Oatmeal and Vanilla Rye (see p. 202)

½ ounce pure maple syrup

dash Fee Brothers old-fashioned bitters

8 drops Bittercube Blackstrap bitters

In a mixing glass full of ice, stir ingredients except bitters until maple syrup blends. Strain into rocks glass full of ice. Add bitters around rim.

	NAME	Above the Daily Hum		
	SPIRIT	Whiskey	GLASS	Martini
	CREATOR	Shawn Jones		

Ingredients

2 ounces rye

1 ounce Navan vanilla cognac

1 ounce Hum liqueur

8 drops Bittercube orange bitters

Griottine or other brandied cherry

In a mixing glass filled with ice, stir all liquid ingredients except bitters until cold. Strain into martini glass and add bitters around rim. Garnish with brandied cherry.

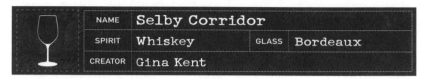

NAME	Selby Corridor		
SPIRIT	Whiskey	GLASS	Bordeaux
CREATOR	Gina Kent		

Ingredients

1½ ounces Coffee Rye (see p. 202)

¾ ounce Amaro Averna

½ ounce Dubonnet Rouge

¼ ounce Hazelnut Orgeat (see p. 185)

2 dashes orange bitters

Lagavulin single-malt scotch

Rinse bordeaux wineglass with scotch, discarding excess. Stir remaining ingredients with ice and strain into wineglass.

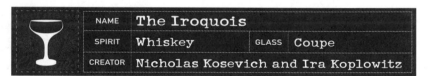

NAME	The Iroquois		
SPIRIT	Whiskey	GLASS	Coupe
CREATOR	Nicholas Kosevich and Ira Koplowitz		

Ingredients

2 ounces Buffalo Trace bourbon

¾ ounce fresh lemon juice

¾ ounce Demerara Syrup (see p. 181)

1 drop Terra Spice birch extract

St-Germain elderflower liqueur

Rinse coupe with St-Germain, discarding excess. Shake remaining ingredients with ice and strain into coupe.

	NAME	Of the Older Fashion		
	SPIRIT	Whiskey	GLASS	Rocks
	CREATOR	Nicholas Kosevich and Ira Koplowitz		

Ingredients

2 ounces Old Weller Antique bourbon

½ (light) ounce Muscovado Syrup (see p. 187)

15 drops Bittercube cherry bark–vanilla bitters

11 drops Bittercube orange bitters

9 drops Bittercube Bolivar bitters

grapefruit peel coin

In a mixing glass filled with ice, stir all liquid ingredients. Strain into rocks glass filled with ice or with one large ice chunk. Squeeze grapefruit coin over cocktail and drop in.

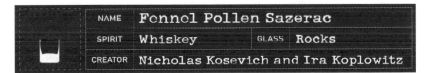

	NAME	Fennel Pollen Sazerac		
	SPIRIT	Whiskey	GLASS	Rocks
	CREATOR	Nicholas Kosevich and Ira Koplowitz		

Ingredients

2 ounces Willett rye

½ ounce Fennel Pollen Syrup (see p. 186)

21 drops Bittercube orange bitters

St. George's absinthe

lemon peel coin

Rinse chilled rocks glass with absinthe, discarding excess. Stir remaining liquid ingredients with ice and strain into glass. Squeeze lemon coin over cocktail and drop in.

NORTH STAR COCKTAILS

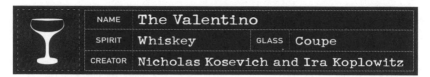

NAME	The Valentino		
SPIRIT	Whiskey	GLASS	Coupe
CREATOR	Nicholas Kosevich and Ira Koplowitz		

Ingredients

¾ ounce Dewar's White Label scotch

¾ ounce Cherry Heering

¾ ounce Carpano Punt e Mes vermouth

¾ ounce orange juice (plus dash simple syrup, if juice isn't
   sweet enough)

18 drops Bittercube orange bitters

sour French cherry

Shake lightly liquors, juice, and 15 drop of the bitters with ice and strain into coupe. Garnish with cherry and remaining 3 drops of bitters.

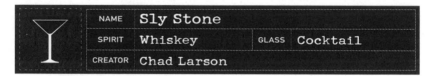

NAME	Sly Stone		
SPIRIT	Whiskey	GLASS	Cocktail
CREATOR	Chad Larson		

Ingredients

1½ ounces Rittenhouse 100-proof rye

½ ounce Zirbenz Stone pine liqueur

½ ounce St. Elizabeth Allspice Dram

½ ounce Rothman & Winter apricot liqueur

4 drops Bittercube Blackstrap bitters

Stir ingredients with ice and strain into chilled cocktail glass.

Absinthe misting of a Sazerac glass

	NAME	Dread Gaelic		
	SPIRIT	Whiskey	GLASS	Rocks
	CREATOR	Dan Oskey		

Ingredients

2 ounces Dewar's blended scotch

½ ounce Gosling's or other
dark rum

½ ounce Grand Marnier

¼ ounce Licor 43

4 dashes Cacao Bean Bitters
(see p. 193)

brandied cherry

Shake liquid ingredients with ice and pour contents into rocks glass. Garnish with cherry.

NAME	The Passenger		
SPIRIT	Whiskey	GLASS	Rocks
CREATOR	Michael Rasmussen		

Ingredients

1½ ounces rye

1 ounce Campari

¼ ounce Luxardo amaro

½ ounce Luxardo maraschino liqueur

orange peel coin

To a rocks glass, add liquid ingredients, stir, and add ice. Squeeze orange coin over cocktail and drop in.

NAME	Lane Zamprey		
SPIRIT	Whiskey	GLASS	Coupe
CREATOR	Jeff Rogers		

Ingredients

1½ ounces rye

½ ounce Grand Marnier

¼ ounce Fernet-Branca

½ ounce amber agave nectar

½ ounce fresh-squeezed lemon juice

2 dashes Regan's orange bitters

½ pasteurized egg white

lemon twist

Place liquid ingredients in a shaker and cap. Shake hard 10 seconds. Remove cap and fill with ice. Shake hard 25 to 30 seconds. Strain with a Hawthorn strainer and a fine-mesh strainer into chilled coupe and garnish with lemon twist.

NAME	Manhattan		
SPIRIT	Whiskey	GLASS	Rocks
CREATOR	Peder Schweigert		

Ingredients

2 ounces Willett rye

1 ounce Sweet Cedar Vermouth (see p. 207)

8 drops Bittercube Bolivar bitters

orange twist

3 Preserved Cherries, on a skewer (see p. 208)

Stir rye and vermouth in an ice-filled pint glass until liquid level increases by 2 ounces. Strain into an ice-filled rocks glass. Garnish with orange twist, capturing orange oil on top of drink. Insert skewered cherries into drink and top with bitters.

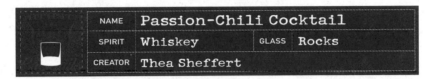

NAME	Passion-Chili Cocktail		
SPIRIT	Whiskey	GLASS	Rocks
CREATOR	Thea Sheffert		

Ingredients

- 1½ ounces Maker's Mark bourbon
- 1½ ounces Passion Fruit–Chili Mix (see below)
- cold club soda
- orange wheel

Shake vigorously bourbon and Passion Fruit–Chili Mix with ice. Pour contents into rocks glass and top with club soda. Garnish with orange wheel.

Passion Fruit—Chili Mix

Ingredients

- 1¾ cups Boiron passion fruit purée
- 1 cup sugar
- ¾ cup fresh lime juice
- 3 to 4 Thai chilies, halved

Heat all ingredients until sugar dissolves. Strain out chilies after base has chilled or leave in until desired heat is achieved. Store in a sealed container and keep refrigerated.

Wine, Sparkling Wine, and Liqueur Cocktails

NAME	The Biting of the Apple		
SPIRIT	Sparkling	GLASS	Champagne
CREATOR	Johnny Michaels		

When I was living in the big *Addams Family* party house, I had several roommates, and I think I was the only one who had never seen any ghosts, which disappointed me because I thought it'd be cool to, you know, say, "Hey, what's up ghosts? Make yourselves comfortable. Do whatever you want. Just don't be messing with my dogs, or I'll light up a smudge stick on your ass!" I cleansed the house several times after weird incidents in which the dogs barked at an empty corner of a room. Anyway, one time I had the living room to myself late at night, and I was watching *Blue Velvet* on cable TV. It got to the part where the young kid was getting it on with Isabella Rossellini, and she was asking him to hit her, and he was like, what the hell? But she was insistent, and right before he gave in and did it, I clearly heard, right in my right ear, "Bite the apple." You want to talk about goose bumps?

This drink is a variation of a cognac champagne cocktail that uses calvados instead of cognac and a hint of pomegranate, which makes it a pretty red color and appeals to the ladies—always a good idea.

Ingredients

¾ ounce calvados

½ ounce apple schnapps

½ ounce Pama pomegranate
     liqueur (so embarrassing)

4 ounces cava (approximately)

dash unsweetened pomegranate
     juice

lemon wedge

sugar

small apple slice

Rub lemon wedge around top inch of a champagne flute and coat with sugar. Shake liquid ingredients, except cava, in a cobbler shaker with ice and double strain into flute. Pour in cava, but don't pour too fast, because the drink has creeper foam, which'll sneak up on you and overflow. Mount the apple slice at an angle, so that there's room to sip.

WINE & LIQUEUR

NORTH STAR COCKTAILS

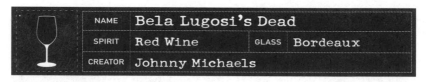

NAME	Bela Lugosi's Dead		
SPIRIT	Red Wine	GLASS	Bordeaux
CREATOR	Johnny Michaels		

This Halloween drink is named after the Bauhaus song, in case you don't know. It was inspired by Barolo Chinato, an Italian wine-based digestif that I'd read about a couple years ago but couldn't source for a reasonable cost, so I decided to try to make up something similar. I serve it with a chunk of dark Valrhona chocolate, and people take sips and nibbles in the candlelight. They talk softly while gazing into each other's eyes, unknowingly surrounded by spirits, who listen to everything they say.

Ingredients

3 ounces big Italian red wine
¾ ounce 20-year tawny port
¾ ounce Unicum Zwack

Just pour into a bordeaux wineglass and swirl to mix. Serve with a nice chunk of dark chocolate.

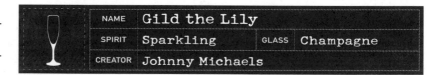

NAME	Gild the Lily		
SPIRIT	Sparkling	GLASS	Champagne
CREATOR	Johnny Michaels		

I suggest making a bottle of the mix and keeping it refrigerated, not for perishability's sake but for ease of making future cocktails. It's a great spring, summer party cocktail.

Ingredients

1 ounce Gild the Lily Mix (see below)
4 or 5 ounces cava (approximately)
lemon peel spiral

Pour chilled mix into champagne flute with a sugared rim and top with cava. Garnish with lemon spiral.

Gild the Lily Mix

Ingredients

4 ounces gin

3 ounces Yellow Chartreuse

3 ounces St-Germain elderflower liqueur

2 ounces Monin lavender syrup

$\frac{1}{8}$ ounce orange flower water

$\frac{1}{4}$ ounce orange bitters

Mix and store in a sealed bottle. Makes enough for about 10 cocktails.

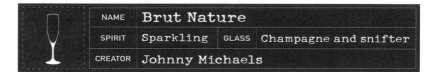

NAME	Brut Nature		
SPIRIT	Sparkling	GLASS	Champagne and snifter
CREATOR	Johnny Michaels		

This one could be accurately described as a deconstructed champagne cocktail, if I wanted to be a wiener about it. By separating the main elements of this cocktail, the differences in their personalities are magnified. The velvet heroin luxury of the cognac contrasts with the bracing, invigorating champagne.

Ingredients

$1\frac{1}{2}$ ounces cognac

$\frac{1}{2}$ ounce Luxardo maraschino liqueur

2 dashes Fee Brothers old-fashioned bitters

champagne

Add cognac, Luxardo, and bitters to snifter and swirl to combine. Fill champagne flute two-thirds full of cava or champagne.

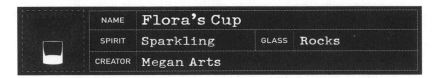

NAME	Flora's Cup		
SPIRIT	Sparkling	GLASS	Rocks
CREATOR	Megan Arts		

Ingredients

1½ ounces Aperol
1½ ounces Cinzano Bianco vermouth
1 to 2 drops orange flower water
3 raspberries
2 orange slices
2 to 3 ounces prosecco
edible nasturtium blossom (optional)

To a rocks glass with ice, add all liquids, except prosecco, and raspberries and orange slices. Briefly stir and top with prosecco. If so inclined, garnish with spicily scented, edible nasturtium blossom.

NAME	Kir Rose		
SPIRIT	Sparkling	GLASS	Champagne
CREATOR	Pip Hanson		

Ingredients

¼ ounce Luxardo maraschino liqueur
¼ ounce Monin strawberry syrup
rosé prosecco or champagne
orange twist

Fill chilled champagne flute halfway with sparkling rosé. Add Luxardo and strawberry syrup. Top with sparkling rosé and garnish with orange twist.

NAME	Behind Blue Eyes		
SPIRIT	Red Wine	GLASS	Bordeaux
CREATOR	Pip Hanson		

Ingredients

- 2 liters Noilly Prat sweet vermouth
- 1 bottle red table wine
- 12 ounces gin
- 12 ounces Luxardo maraschino liqueur
- 1 ounce orange bitters
- $\frac{1}{2}$ ounce orange flower water
- 2 lemons, thinly sliced
- 1 orange, thinly sliced

Add lemon and orange slices to a large pitcher and pour in remaining ingredients. Refrigerate overnight to marry ingredients. Serve over ice in bordeaux wineglasses.

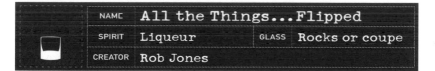

NAME	All the Things...Flipped		
SPIRIT	Liqueur	GLASS	Rocks or coupe
CREATOR	Rob Jones		

Ingredients

- 1 ounce Fernet-Branca
- 1 ounce Green Chartreuse
- $\frac{1}{4}$ ounce Cynar
- $\frac{3}{4}$ ounce simple syrup (see p. 181)
- $\frac{1}{4}$ ounce heavy cream
- 1 egg
- $\frac{1}{4}$ ounce Angostura bitters

Shake all ingredients without ice. Add ice and shake again, viciously. Serve in rocks glass or coupe—whatever, really, as long as there's no ice or straws.

NAME	I've Never Heard of This!		
SPIRIT	Liqueur	GLASS	Cocktail
CREATOR	Chad Larson		

Ingredients

1½ ounces Zirbenz Stone pine liqueur

¾ ounce Fernet-Branca

½ ounce Nux Alpina walnut liqueur

¾ ounce agave nectar

Shake vigorously all ingredients with ice and double strain into chilled cocktail glass.

NAME	A Perfect Ending		
SPIRIT	Liqueur	GLASS	Coupe
CREATOR	Tim Leary		

A light after-dinner dessert drink. A little espresso to get you through the night and a little sweetness for a great liquid dessert.

Ingredients

1 ounce Cherry Heering

1 ounce Nocello walnut liqueur

1 egg

2 ounces room-temperature espresso

dash ground allspice

Shake egg only vigorously without ice. Add remaining ingredients and ice, stir, and strain into coupe.

WINE & LIQUEUR

NORTH STAR COCKTAILS

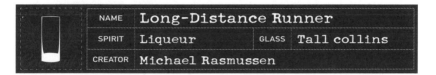

NAME	Prince of Darkness		
SPIRIT	Sparkling	GLASS	Champagne
CREATOR	Michael Rasmussen		

Ingredients

1 ounce Navan vanilla cognac

champagne

sugar cube

2 dashes Angostura bitters

Soak sugar cube with bitters. Pour vanilla cognac into champagne flute and fill glass with champagne, leaving room for sugar cube. Drop in sugar cube.

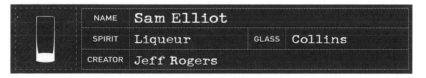

NAME	Long-Distance Runner		
SPIRIT	Liqueur	GLASS	Tall collins
CREATOR	Michael Rasmussen		

Ingredients

2 ounces Fernet-Branca

2 ounces Lemon Sour (see p. 189)

2 ounces kombucha tea

3 blood orange slices

Muddle blood orange slices in tall collins glass. Add ice and remaining ingredients and stir.

NAME	Sam Elliot		
SPIRIT	Liqueur	GLASS	Collins
CREATOR	Jeff Rogers		

Ingredients

1½ ounces Jägermeister

1 teaspoon toasted sesame seeds

3 ounces small-batch root beer

Muddle Jägermeister and sesame seeds in a shaker. Fill two-thirds with ice, cap, and shake. Strain with a Hawthorn strainer and a fine-mesh strainer into an ice-filled collins glass and top with root beer.

NAME	King Cobra		
SPIRIT	Liqueur	GLASS	Martini
CREATOR	Geoffrey Trelstad and Sonya Runkle		

Offer this aperitif at your next dinner party.

Ingredients

½ ounce Beefeater gin
½ ounce açaí berry liqueur
rosé cava
mint sprig
maraschino cherry

Shake vigorously gin and liqueur with ice and strain into chilled martini glass. Top with cava and garnish with mint sprig and cherry.

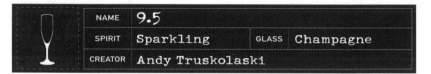

NAME	9.5		
SPIRIT	Sparkling	GLASS	Champagne
CREATOR	Andy Truskolaski		

Ingredients

3 ounces Astoria 9.5 prosecco
¾ ounce Pearl cucumber vodka
½ ounce St-Germain elderflower liqueur
½ ounce simple syrup (see p. 181)
½ ounce fresh lime juice
lemon peel coin
cranberry

Shake vigorously all liquid ingredients except prosecco and strain into champagne flute. Add prosecco and garnish with lemon peel skewered with cranberry.

NAME	Lychee or Love It		
SPIRIT	Liqueur	GLASS	Martini
CREATOR	Andy Truskolaski		

Ingredients

1 ounce Crème Yvette liqueur

1 ounce cranberry juice

½ ounce fresh lime juice

½ ounce simple syrup (see p. 181)

3 sprigs rosemary

1 lychee fruit (blanched or canned)

lime wedge

Lavender Sugar (see below)

Rub half of chilled martini glass rim with lime wedge and coat with Lavender Sugar. Strip rosemary sprig and add leaves and lychee to a Boston shaker. Muddle rosemary and lychee, add liquid ingredients, and add ice and shake. Strain into martini glass.

Lavender Sugar

Ingredients

¼ cup culinary lavender buds

½ cup powdered sugar

½ cup granulated sugar

Mix in a food processor. Sift sugar mixture in a sifter or in a bowl with a whisk. Store in an airtight container.

The Expanded
Cocktail List

At La Belle Vie we have two drink lists. The first is a little one that goes out to every table and lists our wines by the glass and my starting lineup of cocktails. This lineup is about half full-time players and half seasonal specialists, with a rookie or two mixed in, usually around thirteen or fourteen total. The second is an expanded cocktail list, which has another forty or so options that do not rely on seasonal, perishable house-made syrups and which we give out to our guests when we can tell they are digging our little drink list. Giving everyone a massive sixty-drink list right off the bat would be too much, since people are excited and overly stimulated sometimes when they first arrive, taking things in and talking to their friends. I consider the expanded list to be my bench players, subbing them in and out during the year. People are always asking when their favorite seasonal drink will be available. They look forward to its appearance and lament when its shift is over. My goal is to come up with one keeper per season. It might not sound like much, but you end up with a cool roster over time.

The expanded list also has some conceptual drinks, cocktails that don't exist but are meant to be read as entertainment, that are meant to be funny or thought provoking. I love it when people are laughing and enjoying themselves just reading the drink names and descriptions, before they even see or taste the cocktail they have chosen.

You Can't Tell Me, Because I Already Know (aka You're Ruining My Life)
This one's a can of Red Bull, no glass. We don't even have Red Bull at La Belle Vie. No matter where I hide it, the FoodCookers will find it. I think they hire their interns based on their Red Bull–sniffing abilities. I can't afford to have it around. I don't have any children, but I figure whoever might have teenagers would instantly get this joke drink.

Yes, I'm Afraid I Must Insist
This one's just a vodka and Red Bull—price listed at fifteen dollars. I put a little caption next to the price that reads, "Yes, I'm afraid we must insist." Of course if someone ordered it (and we actually had Red Bull), I wouldn't stick it to them like that. If that was what they wanted, then I would make it for them with no attitude. But we don't have it.

Seen Your Video
Back in the 1980s when Hüsker Dü, The Replacements, and Soul Asylum were all coming up, I felt Minneapolis held the title—the belt—for a while, anyway, of best rock city in the country, if not the world. Nobody could match the power of those three bands at the same time and place. And if you didn't know, we beat Seattle to the punch. Anyway, The Replacements have a song called "Seen Your Video," with the lines: "Seen your video, / It's phony rock and roll / We don't want to know." And in their honor, this drink, a bottle of Grain Belt Premium and a shot of Jim Beam, gives the middle finger to all the fancy cocktails on the list. (My debauched youth was filled with shots of Jameson and Jim Beam, with the occasional beer to wash them down. I've actually never had a proper Martini—the ironies of life.) A lot of people, especially the younger ones, laugh at this drink's description, but I can tell they have no idea what they're laughing at, so I explain to them a bit about our rich local music history.

I Was Meaning to Do That
This one has no description. It's worth nothing, so it costs nothing. People ask what's it's about, and I tell them it can mean different things to different people, like don't put off something important, because the thief in the night often comes by surprise, whether it's charity work, a dream vacation, or quitting a bad habit. It could mean lots of things. Also, sometimes a person can get sick of hearing excuses. I don't always get everything done that I want to or say that I will get done, but I usually follow up those moments with, "It's too bad for me that excuses don't count."

Honus Wagner (garnish)
Honus Wagner was an all-star baseball player way back in the day—way, way back. Some tobacco company decided they were going to include collectable baseball cards in their chewing tobacco. Honus apparently was anti-tobacco and forbade the company from using his card in the promo. A few cards had already made it out, though, which consequently made them the rarest baseball cards ever produced.

I made some funny homemade collectable cards of the lounge staff at La Belle Vie: the cocktailers, bartenders, barbacks, hostesses. I took pictures, printed them up, glued them to thin, hard-cut posterboard, wrapped them in wax paper with a stick of gum. It was a lot of work. They were a one-dollar add-on to any drink on our list. I think we ended up selling three or four of them, which made everything ironically appropriate. I figure someday I'll be rummaging through my clutter collection, trying to find things I can stand parting with, find the box with all the unwrapped cards, and enjoy the trip down memory lane.

The rarest of all cards is SvedkaMan. Eric the Barback became SvedkaMan the night he was moping around at work after breaking up with his girlfriend the night before. He came up to the bar, hanging his head, and held up the two bottles of Svedka vodka we had sent him to get, one in each hand, so we could lift the bar top flipper for him. The other bartender and I just burst out laughing, and from then on, to his chagrin, he was SvedkaMan. SvedkaMan was kind enough to re-create the moment, months later, after he had left La Belle Vie's employ, for picture-taking and card-making purposes. I think he and I are the only people who have his card.

The Wisdom of the Centuries

I know this French guy who stops by from time to time, usually waiting for a moment when we're struggling to keep up with the nonstop drink-order machine to ask us to make him something special (yes, you, Nico). We love doing this type of thing, just not when our hair is on fire and the boat is springing leaks faster than we can bail water. Anyway, one day, on a slow night (thank god), he was going off about how much he loved lemon in his water, and it got me thinking. I'm interested in Masonic things and such and had recently heard the phrase "the wisdom of the centuries," and I wondered if perhaps water with lemon might have been the first cocktail ever invented. I imagined some caveman handing it to his buddy and saying, "Yo, dude, try this." The drink description is chilled water, no ice, with lemon, and it's free.

General Jack D. Ripper

People sometimes ask me what my favorite drink on the menu is, and while I don't really have one, if forced I'd have to pick this one because, to my knowledge, it's never been ordered in the three years it's been listed. It's named after the crazy general from *Dr. Strangelove*. It's just a glass of distilled water (substituted for rainwater), no ice.

The Agony of Defeat

I made this one the day after watching the Minnesota Vikings lose the nail-biting overtime heartbreaker to the New Orleans Saints in the 2009 NFC Championship game. That one ranks a close second to the Vikings' overtime loss to the Atlanta Falcons in the 1998 NFC Championship game in my book. This was the first time

I ever tried to make a truly nasty drink, except, I suppose, the ridiculous birthday shots people wanted for their friends when I worked at Gluek's. I used to ask them, "Is this guy screwing your girlfriend or what?" I took pride in making a drink that looked horrible and delighted the onlookers but actually wasn't so bad for the birthday person.

I made this one drink, The Ashtray Shot, that was a big crowd pleaser. This was a while ago, back when people could smoke in bars. (Hell, it seems unbelievable now, but I remember being able to smoke behind the bar while working!) I'd take a clean glass ashtray, add a half ounce whiskey and a half ounce Goldschläger, and top it with two or so ounces of tap hard cider. Then, I'd find someone smoking at the bar and ask them to flick a piece of ash into it. It looked terrible but actually wasn't bad. You surprisingly couldn't really taste the ash.

Anyway, for The Agony of Defeat, I wanted something so heinous that you would never forget it, much like the heartbreak of watching the Vikings lose those two games. I don't have exact measurements for this one, so I will give you my best recollection. I took an empty, label-free bottle and filled it only halfway. It was about 40 percent Cruzan blackstrap molasses rum, 30 percent Bacardi 151 rum, 10 percent blackstrap molasses, 10 percent Laphroaig single-malt scotch, and 10 percent crème de banana. Then I hit it with some salt solution and some crushed–red pepper tincture.

I put it on the drink list. It was a conceptual drink I didn't expect to sell but surprisingly sold plenty. I would pour about a half ounce in a small shot glass and microwave it for six seconds to make it extra fumy. Terrible, just terrible, terrible. But surprisingly, people liked it in a weird way—like a movie sooo bad it becomes funny and good. I remember this group of three super-straight, younger, white-bread couples getting three shots and sharing each one. Then one of the young ladies announced she kind of liked it, and her mortified boyfriend looked at her like she just announced she loved getting [CENSORED]. I've always wondered if they broke up over that. The drink smelled like a wet, nasty, ACE bandage, just a terrible, terrible taste that will never be forgotten, much like the memory of those two football games.

Psycho Tiki Warlords from Outer Space
This last one, I admit, is out there. People keep trying to talk me out of it, but I'm just super into the idea of a drink being a physical artifact tied to a piece of fiction. Proof Drink Design was hired to design new drinks for Psycho Suzi's, a popular tiki bar in Northeast Minneapolis that moved to a bigger location in the fall of 2010.

In the end, almost all of the drinks they picked were created by their own bartenders. For the record, this drink and the story behind it are all mine. Pip Hanson had nothing to do with any of it (let's just say he doesn't care for it and leave it at that). So now that that is clear, I can tell you about it.

The Psycho Tiki Warlords from Outer Space are human-machine hybrids of Polynesian decent that can exist in space and on Earth's surface. Eight of these creatures are defending Earth from other alien races that want something from us or seek to conquer the entire planet for themselves. The warlords take turns going on leave to a remote island in the Pacific, where they drink an intoxicating liquid out of pressurized cans. This liquid is lethal to humans: I am the only person to ever taste it and survive. The human-safe cocktail I created tastes somewhat like the real thing, only much, much milder. These cocktails—half liquor, half beer—are meant to be served in collectable pint glasses displaying the different warlord characters. The first one, Chief Alphazom, was created by Minneapolis graphic artist Josh Grzybowski.

The idea was that whenever the Earth came under attack, maybe once a week or so, an alarm would sound and an announcement would be made at the bar. After ten to fifteen minutes, another announcement would relay that the PTWFOS had defeated the invaders who wanted our planet for themselves and there would be a celebratory drink special the rest of the night. Woo-hoo! Every now and then, a warlord would die in battle, and a new character—and a new glass—would take his place. The retired glasses would become extra valuable to collectors. Patrons could also visit the Psycho Suzi's website—maybe on their smartphones while at the bar and drinking a PTWFOS cocktail—and read the different characters' bios to learn what kind of modern Earth music they like, their favorite foods, or their dating preferences (the PTWFOS have a large groupie following among the locals on the island).

If you want to read the full-on crazy story, go to psychotikiwarlordsfromouterspace.com. I still really like this kitschy concept and hope it ends up being served someday. When someone smacks the table, looks me dead in the eye, and says they want a really whacked-out, original drink idea, I just smile, lean over, and open my metal briefcase.

Nonalcoholic Refreshments

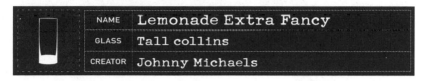

NAME	Lemonade Extra Fancy
GLASS	Tall collins
CREATOR	Johnny Michaels

Ingredients

1 ounce cold Moon Mix (see p. 47)

5 ounces cold club soda (approximately)

lemon wheel

To an ice-filled tall collins glass, add club soda and top with Moon Mix. Insert straw, stir, and then add lemon wheel.

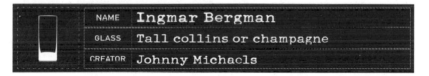

NAME	Ingmar Bergman
GLASS	Tall collins or champagne
CREATOR	Johnny Michaels

Ingredients

1 ounce White Grape Sour (see p. 191)

5 ounces cold club soda (approximately)

lemon wheel or lemon twist

To an ice-filled tall collins glass or chilled champagne flue, add soda and sour and stir. Insert lemon wheel or garnish with twist.

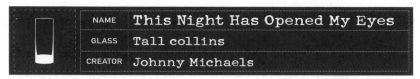

NAME	**This Night Has Opened My Eyes**
GLASS	Tall collins
CREATOR	Johnny Michaels

Ingredients

½ ounce San Pellegrino Sanbittèr

½ ounce Concord grape juice concentrate, defrosted

½ ounce Lemon Sour (see p. 189)

2 ounces cold club soda (approximately)

2 ounces tonic water (approximately)

½ orange wheel

To an ice-filled tall collins glass, add ingredients and stir. Garnish by inserting half orange wheel.

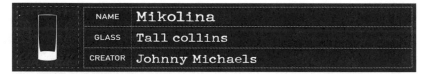

NAME	**Mikolina**
GLASS	Tall collins
CREATOR	Johnny Michaels

Ingredients

½ ounce San Pellegrino Sanbittèr   5 ounces cold club soda

1 ounce Lemon Sour (see p. 189)   (approximately)

lemon wheel

To an ice-filled tall collins glass, add liquid ingredients and stir. Insert straw and lemon wheel.

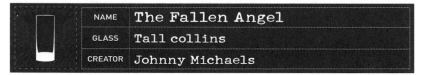

NAME	**The Fallen Angel**
GLASS	Tall collins
CREATOR	Johnny Michaels

Ingredients

dash Fee Brothers old-fashioned bitters

dash Angostura bitters

NONALCOHOLIC

NORTH STAR COCKTAILS

3 dashes orange bitters

1 tablespoon Habanero-Butterscotch Syrup (see p. 183)

Sprite

cold club soda

blood orange (when in season) or orange slice

To an ice-filled tall collins glass, add bitters and syrup. Fill half remaining volume with half Sprite and half club soda and mix with a straw. Then top off glass with half Sprite and half club soda and insert blood orange or orange slice to garnish.

NAME	**Watermelon Pickle Pop**
GLASS	Tall collins
CREATOR	Johnny Michaels

Ingredients

3 ounces Pickled Watermelon Sour (see p. 42)

1½ ounces Sprite

1½ ounces cold club soda

lemon wheel

To an ice-filled tall collins glass, add liquid ingredients and insert lemon wheel.

NAME	**Lydia's Knocked Up**
GLASS	Tall collins
CREATOR	Johnny Michaels

Ingredients

1½ ounces Valentino Mix (see p. 78)

1½ ounces orange juice

1½ ounces cold club soda (approximately)

1½ ounces Sprite (approximately)

4 or 5 apple slices

To an ice-filled tall collins glass, add liquid ingredients and stir. Insert apple slices.

Homemade Syrups, Bitters, Infusions, and More

Syrups and Sours

Simple Syrup

The most basic recipe for simple syrup is 1 part sugar to 1 part water. I think that's too watery, though. You can go 2 to 1, which some of the other recipe contributors prefer, but that's a little heavy for me. I use 3 parts sugar to 2 parts water, by volume. You can add a touch of corn syrup or expensive and hard-to-source glucose to avoid any crystallization. You can use the stuff in a squirt bottle, but if you've made enough to last awhile, store it in the refrigerator in a well-sealed container.

Ingredients

3 cups sugar   2 cups water

Heat sugar and water until sugar dissolves. Remove from heat and let cool. Store in a sealed container and refrigerate.

Demerara Syrup

This simple syrup is made with demerara sugar, not to be confused with brown sugar. For this syrup, use 2 parts sugar to 1 part water. This just has a deeper, richer flavor than regular simple syrup. It's like comparing a hearty artisanal bread to white sandwich bread. They're both good; it just depends on what you're making.

Ingredients

2 cups demerara sugar   1 cup water

Heat sugar and water until sugar dissolves. Remove from heat and let cool. Store in a sealed container and refrigerate.

Brown Sugar Syrup   Thea Sheffert

Ingredients

1 cup brown sugar   1 cup water

Heat on stove until dissolved and then bottle and refrigerate.

Mint Syrup

I use a pound of mint per gallon of simple syrup, but that's way too much for you, so do the math and make what you need. You could make a gallon batch, divide it up, and freeze it in portions. This syrup will lose its flavor and color after a week or so and go bad soon after. I throw mine away as soon as it's not the sweet light-green crude I love.

Ingredients

2 ounces mint leaves   2 cups simple syrup (see p. 181)

Pick through mint leaves, removing stems and dirty, brown, or black leaves, and rinse in cold water. In a metal colander, briefly blanch mint in boiling water. Remove from water and shock mint in a big bowl of ice water. Remove mint and squeeze out most of the water. Add mint and simple syrup to a blender. Blend starting at a low speed and work your way up. You want the mint leaves to be in small bits but not liquefied, so they can be strained later. Transfer to a sealed container and store in refrigerator overnight or up to 2 days, no longer, shaking periodically. Strain syrup through a chinois or a fine-mesh strainer, using a ladle to work all syrup through. Refrigerate in a sealed container.

Ginger Syrup

Ingredients

10 ounces ginger, peeled and   2 cups simple syrup (see p. 181)
chopped   2 cups water (approximately)

Add ginger and simple syrup to a blender. Blend starting at a low speed and work your way up. Do not let ginger liquefy or the resulting syrup will have too much sediment. Add blended syrup to a pot and mix in water. Simmer until added water evaporates. Strain hot syrup through a chinois or a fine-mesh strainer, using a ladle to work all syrup through. Refrigerate in a sealed container.

Apple-Ginger Syrup

Ingredients

6 ounces ginger, peeled and chopped

1½ cups apple juice concentrate, defrosted

1½ cups water

Add ginger and apple juice to a blender. Blend starting at a low speed and work your way up. Do not let ginger liquefy. Add mixture to a pot and mix in water. Simmer until added water evaporates. Strain hot syrup through a chinois or a fine-mesh strainer, using a ladle to work all syrup through. Refrigerate in a sealed container.

Habanero-Butterscotch Syrup

The tricky part of making this syrup is adding the correct number of fresh habaneros—anywhere from 4 to 12. I like habaneros that are slightly older looking (though not rotting), a deeper orange, and a little softer. It's always a good idea to use half the syrup and 3 to 4 peppers in your first attempt at simmering the habaneros; if the mixture turns out too spicy, you can cut it down with extra syrup. If it's not spicy enough, add more peppers and water and repeat cooking process. I recommend wearing latex or other protective rubber gloves when cutting up the peppers and using the utmost care when doing so. Think of this ingredient as raw meat: clean the cutting board, knives—everything—right after using so as to minimize the risk of forgetting what pepper residue is on what and possibly touching your eye (or another body part). Believe me, you will make that mistake only once. When you taste the syrup, it should hit you initially as the right sweet/salty balance, and then the habanero feedback will strike with a nice, even, long sustain without being overpowering. This one takes a shooter's touch.

Ingredients

750 milliliters Monin butterscotch syrup

4 to 12 habanero peppers, seeded, deveined, and minced

3 tablespoons kosher salt

To a large pot, add syrup, tap water (about half the syrup amount), and minced peppers. Because these higher-sugar syrups can really inflate and easily boil over amazingly fast, the pot should be no less than one-quarter and no more than one-half full.

Simmer slowly, about 10 to 15 minutes, keeping an eye out for dramatic and quick inflation. The goal is to slowly cook off the added water, so when you strain the mixture and funnel it back into its storage bottle, it matches the original volume. Remove from heat and add salt; about a teaspoon per 6 ounces is a good starting point. Strain hot syrup through a chinois or a fine-mesh strainer to remove pepper pieces, using a ladle to work all syrup through. Refrigerate in a sealed container. It will last at least a couple weeks, probably much longer, but I go through mine pretty quickly.

Rosemary-Orange Syrup

Ingredients

3 ounces rosemary leaves (from about 4 large stems)

3 ounces Cointreau

6 ounces orange juice concentrate, defrosted

To a blender, ideally one with variable speeds, add rosemary leaves, Cointreau, and orange juice concentrate. Start off slow, and increase blending speed until the leaves are finely shredded but still large enough to strain out through a fine-mesh chinois. Do not liquefy. Refrigerate and infuse at least 1 day before straining out rosemary. Leaving it in too long, though, will cause the rosemary to turn brownish black, which you don't want. Finished syrup must be kept refrigerated.

184

Black Pepper Syrup

Ingredients

4 ounces black peppercorns   2 cups water

1 cup simple syrup (see p. 181)

Grind peppercorns in coffee/spice grinder until medium coarse. Add ground pepper, syrup, and water to a pot and bring to a boil. Simmer until added water evaporates. Remove from heat, let cool, transfer to a covered container, and refrigerate overnight. The next day, reheat syrup with a little water until it evaporates: now your syrup will be easier to strain. Strain through a fine-mesh strainer while stilll warm. Press pepper mash with bottom of a ladle to press out all liquid. Refrigerate syrup in a covered container. Stays good at least 2 weeks, probably longer.

Provençal Syrup

Ingredients

1½ cups Monin black currant
syrup
4 tablespoons dried herbes de
Provence
½ cup water

2 teaspoons kosher salt
1½ cups fresh Lemon Sweet and
Sour
⅓ to ½ cup fresh lemon juice

Simmer syrup, water, and herbs until added water evaporates. Strain out herbs and mix in salt until dissolved. Refrigerate syrup, and when cool, mix in lemon sout and juice. Refrigerate syrup in a covered container.

Coke Syrup

Ingredients

12 ounces Coke

Simmer until reduced to 8 ounces.

Cucumber-Mint-Chamomile Syrup   Adam Harness

Ingredients

1 cup sugar
2 cucumbers, chopped but not
peeled or seeded

1 cup water
1 chamomile tea bag
1 mint tea bag

Place sugar, water, and cucumbers in a medium pot and heat until sugar fully dissolves. Remove from heat and steep mint and chamomile tea bags. As it cools, taste until syrup has reached desired flavor. Remove tea bags and strain syrup through a fine-mesh strainer. Bottle and keep in the refrigerator for up to 3 weeks.

Hazelnut Orgeat   Gina Kent

Ingredients

1 pound hazelnuts
3 cups turbinado or demerara
sugar

1½ cups water
4 or 5 dashes rosewater

Heat oven to 400 degrees. Coarsely crush hazelnuts in a bag with a mallet or pulse briefly in a food processor. Place crushed hazelnuts on a baking sheet in the oven and toast 5 minutes, shaking several times. Place toasted nuts, sugar, and water in a medium pot and bring to a low boil. Reduce heat and simmer 5 minutes. Remove from heat, cover, and refrigerate overnight. Strain though a cheesecloth-lined chinois or other fine-mesh strainer. Repeat if necessary to remove any sediment. Add rosewater and mix. Bottle and store in the refrigerator.

Grenadine   Gina Kent

Ingredients

1 liter pomegranate juice

2 cups sugar

5 wide strips orange peel

1 (10-ounce) bottle pomegranate molasses

pinch kosher salt

Over medium heat, simmer pomegranate juice until half its original volume. Remove from heat, add sugar, and whisk until incorporated. Twist orange peels so that oils are expressed into mixture. Add pomegranate molasses and salt and whisk until incorporated. Pour into a bottle with a cap and store in the refrigerator.

Fennel Pollen Syrup

Nicholas Kosevich and Ira Koplowitz

Ingredients

1 cup water

1 tablespoon fennel pollen

1 cup demerara sugar

Bring water to a boil and remove from heat. Add fennel pollen and steep 5 minutes. Add sugar and whisk until dissolved. Strain through a fine-mesh strainer. There will be fennel pollen particles in this syrup, which will give your cocktail a rustic, unpolished look.

Green Tea Syrup

Nicholas Kosevich and Ira Koplowitz

Ingredients

1 cup water   1 cup sugar
5 green tea bags

Bring water to a boil and then remove from heat. Steep tea 5 minutes, squeeze bags, and discard. Whisk in sugar and let cool. Will keep refrigerated for 1 month.

Muscovado Syrup

Nicholas Kosevich and Ira Koplowitz

Ingredients

1 cup water   1 cup muscovado sugar

Bring water to a simmer and add sugar. Remove from heat and whisk until sugar dissolves. Strain through a fine-mesh strainer and let cool. Will keep refrigerated for 1 month.

Rosemary-Maple Syrup   Dan Oskey

Ingredients

1 cup maple syrup
1 tablespoon fresh rosemary, chopped

Bring syrup and rosemary to a simmer, reduce heat, and cook 5 minutes. Strain into a bottle and refrigerate.

Lemon-Basil Syrup   Richy Rivera

Ingredients

4 cups lemon juice   6 ounces basil leaves
5 cups sugar

Bring lemon juice and sugar to a boil. Tear 4 ounces of the basil and add right after first boil. Simmer 5 to 10 minutes. Remove from heat, let cool to room temperature, and strain. Tear and add the remaining basil. Refrigerate overnight. Strain into a bottle and refrigerate.

Lavender Syrup   Richy Rivera

Ingredients

2 cups sugar

2 cups water

½ cup culinary lavender buds

Bring sugar and water to a simmer and add lavender. Remove from heat and let steep until cool or overnight in the refrigerator. Strain into a bottle and refrigerate.

Pomegranate-Lavender Syrup   Richy Rivera

Ingredients

2 cups Boiron pomegranate purée

1 cup Lavender Syrup (see above)

Mix and store refrigerated in a sealed container.

Ginger-Rosemary Syrup   Richy Rivera

Ingredients

4 cups water

2 cups sugar

6 ounces ginger, peeled and sliced

2 ounces rosemary leaves

Bring water to a boil and add sugar, ginger, and 1 ounce of the rosemary. Simmer 5 to 10 minutes. Remove from heat, let cool to room temperature, and add the remaining rosemary. Refrigerate overnight and then strain. Store bottled in refrigerator.

Fanatical Botanical Syrup   Jeff Rogers

Ingredients

1 cup pure cane sugar

1 cup water

⅛ teaspoon ground licorice root

¼ teaspoon ground angelica root

4 raw almonds, blanched
¼ teaspoon dried lemon peel
10 juniper berries
¼ teaspoon ground orris root

⅛ teaspoon ground cassia bark
4 coriander seeds
5 grains of paradise
4 cubeb berries

Place sugar and water in a medium pot and heat until sugar fully dissolves. Turn heat down to low, add remaining ingredients, and simmer 15 to 20 minutes. Turn off heat and allow mixture to cool to room temperature. Strain through a fine-mesh strainer, removing all particles. Bottle and keep in the refrigerator for up to 3 weeks.

Clove Syrup   Jeff Rogers

Ingredients

1 cup pure cane sugar
1 cup water

4 cloves

Place sugar and water in a medium pot and heat until sugar fully dissolves. Turn heat to low, add cloves, and simmer 15 to 20 minutes. Turn off heat and allow mixture to cool to room temperature. Strain through a fine-mesh strainer, removing all particles. Bottle and keep in the refrigerator for up to 3 weeks.

Lemon or Lime Sour

I start off with a fifty-fifty mix of fresh juice and simple syrup and then taste and adjust as needed. The sugar content of lemons and limes will vary throughout the year, and it seems as if every box of produce we get from our supplier is different every time—from different farms, different parts of the world with different weather. You know what I'm saying. Balance is the goal.

Ingredients

¾ cup fresh lemon or lime juice
¾ cup simple syrup (see p. 181)

Mix and store in a 12-ounce container or squirt bottle. (If using squirt bottle, I like to use masking tape to seal the open tip.) Keep refrigerated.

Apple-Ginger-Lemon Sour

Ingredients

8 ounces Apple-Ginger syrup (see p. 183)

8 ounces Lemon Sour (see p. 189)

2 ounces lemon juice

Combine ingredients and store refrigerated.

Ginger-Lemon Sour

Ingredients

8 ounces Ginger Syrup (see p. 182)   2 ounces lemon juice

8 ounces Lemon Sour (see p. 189)

Combine ingredients and store refrigerated.

Minted Kalamansi Sour

Ingredients

1 cup Boiron kalamansi purée, defrosted

1 cup Mint Syrup (see p. 182)

Combine ingredients and store refrigerated.

Cherry-Lemon Sour

Ingredients

6 ounces Lemon Sour (see p. 189)

6 ounces Adriatic or Marco Polo sour cherry syrup or
    Monin cherry syrup

2–3 ounces lemon juice

$\frac{1}{2}$ ounce Fee Brothers old-fashioned bitters

Combine ingredients and store refrigerated.

Yuzu-Ginger Sour

Ingredients

¾ cup Ginger Syrup (see p. 182)   ¼ cup yuzu juice

Combine ingredients and store refrigerated.

Strawberry-Lemon Sour

Ingredients

6 ounces fresh strawberry juice   4 ounces Lemon Sour (see p. 189)
4 ounces Monin strawberry syrup   2 ounces lemon juice

Combine ingredients and store refrigerated.

Blueberry-Lemon Sour

Ingredients

¾ cup fresh lemon juice   ¾ cup Monin blueberry syrup

Combine ingredients and store refrigerated.

White Grape Sour

Verjus is an acidic juice extracted from unripened grapes.

Ingredients

10 ounces unsweetened white grape juice concentrate, defrosted

10 ounces white verjus

1 teaspoon orange bitters

1 teaspoon lemon bitters

Combine ingredients and store refrigerated.

Clover Honey—Lemon Sour

Ingredients

¾ cup clover honey   ¾ cup fresh lemon juice

Combine ingredients and store refrigerated.

Bitters

Bittercube Basic Aromatic Bitters
Nicholas Kosevich and Ira Koplowitz

Bitters are called such because they are exactly that, bitter to the taste, but they are also much more. Bitters are amalgamations of various seeds, herbs, barks, roots, flowers, leaves, and fruit (or vegetables) that are macerated in high-proof spirits. When we develop bitters recipes, we, in a sense, create a Frankenstein plant, picking and choosing a plethora of ingredients from different sources. Many bitters companies use extracts, oils, and flavorings, which speeds up the production process. Our company, Bittercube, uses only natural ingredients in our maceration process, which means that it can take up to fifty-six days to complete one batch.

Bitters are used sparingly in cocktails because they are highly concentrated. They are diluted in a cocktail, however, thus exposing a delicate balance of flavors. Bittercube bitters are packaged in eyedropper bottles because they are more accurate than dashers and because our bitters are highly concentrated. Generally, a cocktail will need between 13 to 19 drops. Bitters can enhance not only cocktails but also simple highballs, sparkling wine, and beer. Consider bitters to be the spice rack of your home bar.

Creating bitters at home is a subtle art. It takes practice and trial and error. Don't get discouraged if a batch doesn't turn out like you'd hoped. The following is a basic aromatic bitters recipe that can be made as is but also used as the base for a more elaborate recipe. If a batch doesn't turn out, don't dump it. Remacerate it, adjusting whatever flavors seem off or adding altogether new ingredients.

Ingredients

2 cups 100-proof bourbon

2 cups Everclear grain alcohol

1 whole nutmeg, crushed

2 teaspoons black peppercorns

2 tablespoons gentian root

1 tablespoon cardamom pods

2 teaspoons coriander seeds

1 tablespoon caraway seeds

1 cinnamon stick

1 tablespoon grated ginger

1 teaspoon whole allspice

1 teaspoon whole clove

1 whole star anise

1 tablespoon jasmine or other floral tea

½ cup raisins

Peel of 1 lemon, 1 orange, and 1 lime

¾ cup sugar

¼ cup honey

Combine all ingredients, except sugar and honey, in a large mason jar and let sit 21 days, shaking vigorously every day. Strain liquid through a cheesecloth, squeezing as much out of mash as possible, and set aside. Simmer solid mash in a saucepan with 2½ cups of water for 15 minutes. Strain this liquid, discard solids, and add sugar and honey to warmed liquid. Let cool. Add cooled liquid to bitters base and let sit 7 days, shaking vigorously daily. Strain through cheesecloth one more time and then let any sediment settle before transferring into eyedropper bottles.

Cacao Bean Bitters   Dan Oskey

Ingredients

2 teaspoons quassia powder

1 teaspoon gentian root

½ teaspoon whole allspice, crushed

½ teaspoon aniseed

½ teaspoon ground nutmeg

½ teaspoon coriander seed, crushed

2 cups Everclear 190-proof grain alcohol

1½ cups cacao nibs

2 vanilla beans, split lengthwise

½ cup sugar

In a dry pan, lightly toast spices, exc ept cacao and vanilla, over medium heat. Add toasted spices and remaining ingredients, except sugar, to a mason jar. Let sit 3 weeks, agitating jar every day. Strain liquid through a cheesecloth, squeezing as much out of mash as possible, and set aside. Boil solid mash in a saucepan with 2 cups of water. Strain this liquid into bitters base and discard solids. Add sugar to a dry pan and cook over medium-low heat, stirring occasionally, until all sugar has liquefied and turned light to medium brown. Add caramelized sugar to bitters. Filter bitters using a Büchner funnel or coffee filters, to remove fine particles, and transfer into eyedropper or other small bottles.

Black Walnut Bitters   Dan Oskey

Ingredients

3 cups premium black walnuts

2 teaspoons quassia powder

2 teaspoons gentian root

1 tablespoon cardamom pods, crushed

1 teaspoon coriander seeds, crushed

1 teaspoon aniseed

1 teaspoon ginger powder

2½ cups Everclear 190-proof grain alcohol

½ cup sugar

In a dry pan, lightly toast walnuts and spices over medium heat. Add toasted mixture and Everclear to a mason jar. Let sit 3 weeks, agitating jar every day. Strain liquid through a cheesecloth, squeezing as much out of mash as possible, and set aside. Boil solid mash in a saucepan with 2 cups of water. Strain this liquid into bitters base and discard solids. Add sugar to a dry pan and cook over medium-low heat, stirring occasionally, until all sugar has liquefied and turned light to medium brown. Add caramelized sugar to bitters. Filter bitters using a Büchner funnel or coffee filters, to remove fine particles, and transfer into eyedropper or other small bottles.

Caraway Tincture

Ingredients

4 ounces caraway seeds

1½ cups 94-proof Gin (I use Beefeater)

Add ingredients to a mason jar and let sit 5 to 7 days, shaking once or twice a day. Strain through a fine-mesh strainer and store in a sealed glass jar.

Hot Pepper Tincture

Everclear 151-proof grain alcohol is legally available in Minnesota. If you want the 190-proof stuff, you'll have to hike it over to Wisconsin, maybe when you buy your beer for the Sunday game.

Ingredients

4 ounces crushed red pepper

1½ cups Everclear grain alcohol

Add ingredients to a mason jar and let sit 5 to 7 days, shaking once or twice a day. Strain through a fine-mesh strainer and store in a sealed glass jar.

Allspice Tincture

Ingredients

4 ounces whole allspice

1½ cups Mount Gay Eclipse gold rum

Lightly toast allspice in a skillet to activate oils. Then transfer ingredients to a mason jar and let sit 5 to 7 days, swirling daily. Strain through a fine-mesh strainer and store in a sealed glass jar.

Cardamom Tincture

Ingredients

4 ounces black cardamom seeds   1½ cups 80-proof vodka

Add ingredients to a mason jar and let sit 5 to 7 days, shaking daily. Strain through a fine-mesh strainer and store in a sealed glass jar.

Cinnamon Tincture

Ingredients

4 ounces cinnamon stick, smashed into chips (do not pulverize)

1½ cups 80-proof vodka

Add ingredients to a mason jar and let sit 5 to 7 days, shaking daily. Strain through a fine-mesh strainer and store in a sealed glass jar.

Tobacco Tincture

I use affordable yet robust, full-flavored cigars for this tincture. Last time I used Maduros. Note: contains nicotine. Do not serve to recovering smokers.

Ingredients

8 ounces cigar tobacco, shredded   1½ cups 80-proof bourbon

Add ingredients to a mason jar and let sit 5 days, shaking daily. Strain through a fine-mesh strainer and store in a sealed glass jar.

Habanero Tincture   Jesse Held

Ingredients

1 habanero pepper, sliced

375 milliliters Everclear grain alcohol

Add ingredients to a mason jar and let sit 1 week. Strain through a fine-mesh strainer and store in a sealed glass jar.

Coriander Tincture
Nicholas Kosevich and Ira Koplowitz

Ingredients

5 tablespoons whole coriander seeds

14 ounces Everclear grain alcohol or 80-proof vodka

Add Everclear or vodka and coriander seeds to a small glass jar. Shake daily for 2 weeks with Everclear and 4 weeks with vodka. Strain through a fine-mesh strainer and then a cheesecloth. Let sit 1 day and pour off tincture, leaving sediment in bottom of jar. Store in a small bottle.

197

Infusions

Earl Grey Gin

Ingredients

750 milliliters Bombay Sapphire gin

15 grams loose-leaf white tip Earl Grey tea

Pour gin into a clear or semitransparent pitcher, add tea, and stir. Stir every couple minutes, until gin takes on an iced tea color, about 10 to 15 minutes, maybe a bit longer if your tea is not high grade. Although if you're committing an entire bottle of Sapphire to the project, tea probably isn't the place to skimp on quality. My choice is Earl Grey White Tip from TeaSource. The stuff is like Dutch hydroponic. Strain infused gin through a chinois and funnel into gin bottle. Stays good without refrigeration.

Pine Smoke Absinthe

I use little spray bottles that I get at beauty supply stores for $1.39. They are small, the size of a breath spray bottle, and work perfectly. You can spend more money on a fancy atomizer if you want, but once you put absinthe and pine smoke extract into something, you will never be able to use it for anything else, ever. It will be there until its atoms are scrambled by a nuclear event.

Ingredients

2 ounces absinthe (I use Vieux Carré)

13 drops pine smoke extract

Mix and store in spray bottle.

Ancho Tequila

Ingredients

1 liter decent-quality blanco tequila (El Jimador or better)

2 tablespoons ancho pepper powder

Funnel powder into tequila bottle, cap, and shake. Shake a couple times a day for 2 to 4 days. Let bottle sit a day, so powder will settle. Slowly decant infused tequila into a coffee filter-lined chinois. Near the end of pouring, give the bottle a swirl and quickly pour in rest of liquid so that last remaining powder is washed out of bottle. Press ancho powder sludge with a ladle to extract as much liquid as possible. Wash bottle *thoroughly* and then rebottle clarified Ancho Tequila using a funnel. Stays good unrefrigerated.

Cucumber Tequila

Ingredients

750 milliliters tequila

1 cucumber

Slice cucumber on a mandolin if you've got one; otherwise, slice by hand, maybe 1/8-inch thick. Pour tequila into a pitcher and add sliced cucumber. Refrigerate overnight and strain. Funnel back into tequila bottle. Keep refrigerated. Stays good at least a week or two.

Cucumber Gin

Ingredients

750 milliliters New Amsterdam gin

1 cucumber

Slice cucumber on a mandolin if you've got one; otherwise, slice by hand, maybe 1/8-inch thick. Pour gin into a pitcher and add sliced cucumber. Refrigerate overnight and strain. Funnel back into gin bottle. Keep refrigerated. Stays good at least a week or two.

Sugar Plum Brandy

Ingredients

1 liter brandy

1 (7-ounce) bag orange essence dried plums

1 (7-ounce) bag cherry essence dried plums

Combine fruit with brandy in big glass jars, cover, and swirl lightly once a day for a week. Strain contents through chinois and funnel back into brandy bottle. You'll lose around 20 percent of the brandy to the fruit. I hate throwing away those brandy-soaked plums. I wish I knew a pig farmer: I bet it would be fun watching those pigs chowing down on them and loving it.

Chamomile Gin   Birk Stefan Grudem

Ingredients

1 liter gin   4 chamomile tea bags

Add gin and tea bags to a mason jar. Let steep 45 minutes. Remove and discard tea bags.

Ginger Applejack   Pip Hanson

Ingredients

750 milliliters Laird's Bottled-in-Bond applejack

½ pound fresh ginger, peeled and grated

Add ingredients to a mason jar and let sit 3 days. Strain through a coffee filter and funnel back into bottle.

Black Pepper Sambuca   Pip Hanson

Ingredients

750 milliliters Romana sambuca

1 teaspoon ground black pepper

Add ingredients to a mason jar and let sit 15 minutes. Strain through a coffee filter and funnel back into bottle.

Butter-Washed Scotch   Pip Hanson

Ingredients

1 liter Dewar's White Label blended scotch

1 liter Johnny Walker Red blended scotch

2 pounds unsalted butter

Melt butter, taking care not to let it burn. When melted, add butter to a large glass container, along with scotch. Let sit at least 24 hours, shaking periodically. Then refrigerate until butter hardens. Strain mixture through a chinois and then a coffee filter into glass container. Store refrigerated.

Cacao Nib Mezcal   Pip Hanson

Ingredients

1 liter Sombra or other smoky mezcal

8 ounces ground cacao nibs

Add ingredients to a mason jar and let rest 24 hours. Strain through a coffee filter and funnel back into bottle.

Black Pepper Right Gin   Adam Harness

Ingredients

1 liter Right gin

1 cup black peppercorns

Add peppercorns and gin to a jar and let steep 15 to 20 minutes. Strain through a fine-mesh strainer and funnel back into gin bottle.

Lemongrass-Ginger Tequila   Jesse Held

Ingredients

750 milliliters blanco tequila

1 stalk lemongrass, chopped

4 ounces ginger, peeled and chopped

Add ingredients to a mason jar. Seal and let sit in a cool, dark place 2 weeks. Strain through a chinois or a fine-mesh strainer and funnel back into tequila bottle.

Jalapeño Tequila Shawn Jones

Ingredients

750 milliliters blanco tequila (I use Lunazul or Milagro)

1 jalapeño pepper

Slice jalapeño and add slices and seeds to a mason jar. Pour in tequila. Seal and let sit in a cool, dark place 2 days, longer for a spicier tequila. Agitate daily. Strain through a chinois or a fine-mesh strainer and funnel back into tequila bottle.

Oatmeal and Vanilla Rye Shawn Jones

Ingredients

750 milliliters rye (I use Old Overholt)

3 cups oatmeal (I use Quaker)

1 vanilla bean, split

To a mason jar, add rye and oatmeal. Seal and let sit in a cool, dark place 2 to 3 days, agitating daily. Add vanilla bean and let sit 1 more day. Strain through cheesecloth, pressing to extract all liquid. Funnel back into rye bottle.

Coffee Rye Gina Kent

Ingredients

4 cups rye (Old Overholt is a fine choice)

1 cup coffee beans

To a mason jar, add rye and coffee beans. Seal and let sit 8 hours. Strain and funnel back into rye bottle.

Chai Tea Rum Collin Lace

Ingredients

750 milliliters Cruzan silver rum

5 chai tea bags

To a mason jar, add rum and tea bags. Seal and let sit 8 to 10 hours. Remove and discard tea bags.

Cucumber Vodka

Garrett Nitzchke and Geoffrey Trelstad

Ingredients

1 liter premium vodka

10 cucumbers, peeled and sliced

Add 5 of the cucumbers and vodka to a mason jar. Seal and let sit in refrigerator 3 weeks. Strain, discard cucumbers, and replace with remaining cucumbers. Seal and let sit an additional 3 weeks. Strain vodka and discard cucumbers.

Roasted—Sweet Corn Tequila   Dan Oskey

Ingredients

750 milliliters Suaza Hornitos plata tequila

1½ cups fresh sweet corn kernels

Heat oven to 350 degrees. On a cookie sheet, lightly brown corn. Add corn and tequila to a mason jar and let sit 1 week. Strain through a chinois or a fine-mesh strainer and funnel back into tequila bottle.

Liqueur, Vermouth, and Ginger Beer

Black Walnut Liqueur   Peder Schweigert

Making liqueur isn't so much a set recipe as it is a series of guidelines. The easiest way to explain how to go about doing it is to elaborate on a recipe for one liqueur and allow you to go out and make your own. Liqueur is easy to make. Unlike bitters, vermouth, and fermented beverages, which demand precision and repetition to get a good product, liqueur just takes time and a few good ingredients. The Internet makes it possible to compare recipes, figure out which elements you like, and then put your own spin on them. It is a long process to make the liqueur but very little work. I break recipes into stages, so I can control the additions of flavor and adjust as needed.

One summer, Lenny Russo came to me with a box of black walnuts fresh from his backyard tree. We talked and decided it was time to make *nocino*, a bittersweet, syrupy Italian liqueur. Black walnuts stain almost everything, so make the liqueur on surfaces that you don't care about or that are impervious to staining and store the liqueur in glass. Don't try to cut corners; this recipe doesn't work with dried walnuts, only freshly picked. Pick some black walnuts sometime around late June, when you can still cut them in half easily, skin and all.

Nuts take a long time to extract. For those with less patience, you can extract flavor from most fruits much more quickly. Reduce the time you infuse to 2 to 3 weeks. Sample the product often, until you are happy with what you have made. Nocino tastes great when made with neutral spirits, but oftentimes an overproof spirit and brandy (I always use brandy with cherries and currants) will do the trick.

When tasting a liqueur as it matures, keep in mind that, over time, sugar helps to enhance the flavor significantly, so don't judge its sweetness too early. Never boil your spirits. Instead, if you desire a stronger extraction, try increasing the proof of your spirit. Always check to see if a certain ingredient not commonly ingested is safe to consume. Peach pits contain, for instance, a small amount of cyanide. Fresh herbs will oxidize and taste brown in your spirits, so use dried herbs. Do your research. Most things have been done once before, and others' errors will work in your favor.

The following is a rough recipe for nocino. It's meant as a starting-off point for your own liqueur-making experiments.

Ingredients

    freshly picked black walnuts, quartered
    80-proof vodka
    Everclear 151-proof grain alcohol
    650 grams sugar per liter of liqueur
    ½ cinnamon stick
    2 whole cloves
    bit of orange peel
    bit of lemon peel

Fill mason jar full of quartered walnuts and cover completely with equal parts vodka and Everclear. Let sit 40 days. Strain well and whisk in sugar to taste. Let sit another 40 days, minimum. From this point things can go one of two ways: lightly spiced or heavily spiced. I err on the lightly spiced side of things, only using whole spices for ease of straining. Let spices and liqueur sit and taste daily until you are happy with your creation, then strain. Once strained, place the jar in a dark place and leave it alone until Christmas.

Ginger Beer   Peder Schweigert

This recipe makes approximately 12 (12-ounce) bottles. Buy clear ones—without screw tops—and clean before bottling. You'll need bottle caps and a bottle capper, too. I use an Emily capper. You'll also want a juicer for the ginger.

Ingredients

    4½ cups filtered water
    500 grams sugar
    ½ stick cinnamon
    1½ whole nutmeg seeds, cracked

12 whole allspice

1 whole star anise

2 whole cloves

2 bay leaves

1 package Lalvin EC-1118 champagne yeast (available online and at brewing supply stores)

2½ pounds ginger, peeled, juiced, and strained through a chinois

2½ quarts apple cider, room temperature

Heat water and sugar until it boils, stirring until sugar dissolves completely. Remove from heat and add spices. Cover tightly and let steep 30 minutes. Strain and let cool until spice stock reaches 109 degrees. Add yeast and, without stirring, let sit 15 to 30 minutes. Stir to incorporate yeast. Add ginger juice and apple cider to spice stock. Mix well to distribute the yeast. Using a funnel, fill each bottle. It's important to stir regularly while you fill the bottles to keep the yeast distribution even. Cap bottles and store at about 70 degrees for approximately 16 hours. Refrigerate and use within 2 weeks; bottles will explode if left too long. Don't store the beer at room temperature, because the bottles will spray-coat your room, not that it wouldn't smell great.

Dry Cedar Vermouth   Peder Schweigert

Acquire all of the herbs and spices already dried. I've tried drying some of my own but couldn't get consistent results. It is important to use high-quality ingredients because the market for many of these herbs is unregulated. Find a source you trust and ask questions. I go to Magus Books in Minneapolis, and their knowledge has been crucial in helping develop many products.

Ingredients

½ gram gentian

1 gram wormwood

⅕ gram angelica

2 grams orange peel

2 grams tangerine peel

6 grams red cedar chips ($\frac{1}{8}$-inch thick)

1 gram licorice root

$\frac{1}{2}$ gram dried basil

$\frac{1}{2}$ gram dried thyme

$\frac{1}{2}$ gram dried sage

$\frac{1}{2}$ gram dried oregano

5 grams ginger root ($\frac{1}{8}$-inch dice)

1$\frac{1}{2}$ grams sarsaparilla

1$\frac{1}{2}$ grams sassafras

2 grams quassia

1 liter semidry white table wine

250 milliliters brandy (I've been using E&J VSOP)

Add herbs and one-quarter of the wine to a small, nonreactive saucepan and bring to a gentle simmer, being careful not to scorch the sides of the pan. Remove from heat, cover tightly, and let steep 15 minutes. Strain through a chinois and discard dried herbs. Stir in reserved wine and brandy, funnel into a large jar, and refrigerate. Vermouth tastes best after it has rested for at least 12 hours. Use within a month, and please keep refrigerated.

Sweet Cedar Vermouth   Peder Schweigert

Ingredients

12 ounces prune juice

3 cups Dry Cedar Vermouth (approximately; see opposite page)

Bring juice to a simmer in a small, nonreactive saucepan and reduce to approximately 4 ounces, or until it forms a molasses-like consistency when cold. Refrigerate molasses and when cold vigorously stir into dry vermouth until fully incorporated. I typically add about 1½ ounces molasses to 8 to 10 ounces dry vermouth. Again, keep refrigerated.

Preserved Cherries   Peder Schweigert

Ingredients

300 grams dried tart cherries, pitted

300 milliliters Dolin sweet vermouth

300 milliliters E&J VSOP brandy

250 grams sugar

2 bay leaves

Combine all ingredients in a nonreactive saucepan big enough to leave 2 inches of room between the top of the pan and the top of the liquid. Bring to a simmer and turn down heat to just maintain the simmer. Keep on the heat until the cherries plump. Store in a sealed container and refrigerate.

North Star Bartenders' Guild Biographies

Johnny Michaels

Johnny Michaels has had a wide variety of jobs over the years, including ice cream man, day laborer, flower shop arranger, graveyard shift gas station attendant, bass player, and union construction worker. He has been working in the bar business for over twenty years and has been employed everywhere from 3.2 beer joints to James Beard Award-winning restaurants. He currently runs (and has since it relocated to Minneapolis from Stillwater) the bar and cocktail program at La Belle Vie. He also created the initial cocktail lists for Café Maude, Barrio I and II, Masu Sushi and Robata, Smalley's Caribbean Barbeque and Pirate Bar, and Icehouse. He's won several bartender of the year awards and was once referred to as bartender of the decade in a local magazine (no, it wasn't the Onion). He won the local Bombay Sapphire Most Inspired Bartender contest in 2008. He writes a monthly article for Mpls.St.Paul Magazine. His current plan is to explore opening a cocktail catering business or a cocktail bar that has an animal charity focus to it. Any interested investors should contact him at jmiko@visi.com.

Johnny Michaels

Megan Arts

Originally hailing from northern Minnesota, Megan has been working behind the bar in Minneapolis since 2007, most recently at Café Maude and now at Marvel Bar. She previously split her time between Minnesota and Wisconsin, where she ran the bar at the Creamery Restaurant and Inn in Downsville for two years. Megan enjoys creating drinks with a whimsical quality that employ quirky herbal liqueurs, bitter aperitifs, and complex vermouths.

Jourdan Gomez

Jourdan represents the Bradstreet Craftshouse in the heart of downtown Minneapolis. Prior to becoming a bartender, he developed his palette working as a barista. While learning how to roast coffee and understanding the feel of weight in a glass and on the tongue, he yearned for a more intoxicating craft. In 2009, he was recruited by master mixologist Toby Maloney and

NORTH STAR COCKTAILS

Megan Arts

Jourdan Gomez

Birk Stefan Grudem

Alchemy Consulting to work at the Bradstreet Craftshouse. He is also a key ingredient in the mix of Metropolis, a Minneapolis-based modern progressive rock band.

Birk Stefan Grudem

Birk has bartended for around seven years at some of the best cocktail bars in town, such as the Town Talk Diner and the Bradstreet Craftshouse. He has studied and learned from the likes of Aaron Johnson, Tim Niver, and Toby Maloney. He is currently taking a break from bartending to launch his new food truck business, Hola Arepa, but it probably won't be long before he is working at another cocktail bar, whether it's his or someone else's.

Pip Hanson

Pip's first night behind a bar was with Johnny Michaels at the Dakota in 2005. After working closely with Johnny for several years, he moved to Tokyo, where he bartended at Fifty One in the Roppongi Hills Club and learned Japanese cocktail technique. Pip also mentored with some of Ginza's master bartenders, including Kazuo Uyeda, the inventor of the Hard Shake. He helped with the translation of the English-language edition of Uyeda's book, *Cocktail Techniques*, as well as Uyeda's first U.S. cocktail seminar in New York City. Pip has worked at cocktail hot spots La Belle Vie, Town Talk Diner, and Café Maude and co-owns a cocktail consulting firm, Proof Drink Design, with Johnny Michaels. He writes a monthly cocktail column for *Metro* magazine and is now running the cocktail program at Marvel Bar.

Adam Harness

Adam started out with craft and classic cocktails at the now-closed Town Talk Diner and is currently the bar manager at Café Maude. He likes to play drums and listen to good music in his spare time.

Pip Hanson

Adam Harness

Jesse Held

Jesse Held

Jesse began in the craft cocktail movement in 2007, sharpening his skills and making his own vermouth, bitters, and seasonal cordials and liqueurs. He has bar managed for cocktail-driven institutions such as the Town Talk Diner and, most recently, the Inn. He has consulted with a host of restaurateurs about their cocktail programs. He created the popular local bartending competition Iron Bartender Minneapolis and most recently joined like-minded bar brethren to form the Midwest's first-ever independent bartender's guild, the North Star Bartenders' Guild, in which he holds the position of president. He is passionate about teaching the local community about cutting-edge classic cocktails. Jesse can now be found working at Marvel Bar with Pip Hanson.

Rob Jones

Rob started his bartending career at Bradstreet Craftshouse and now works at Meritage in St. Paul. He was a chef and cook for twelve years before he switched to bartending. He spent eight years cooking in Phoenix, Arizona, before moving back to his native Twin Cities. He applies the fundamentals he learned in culinary school and in kitchens to his newfound craft.

Shawn Jones

When he was eighteen, Shawn stepped behind the bar and hasn't come out since. He began his serving career as a waiter in his family's New York restaurants after moving to the East Coast from Flint, Michigan. Quickly learning the industry, he arrived in Boston and started bartending in both fine-dining and high-volume establishments. Bored with churning out simple cocktails, he began a study of craft cocktail that he brought with him back to the Midwest. He currently works as the bar manager at Amore Victoria.

Rob Jones

Shawn Jones

Gina Kent

Gina Kent

Gina has been tending bar in the Twin Cities since 2005, most notably honing her skills behind the stick at the Town Talk Diner and the Bradstreet Craftshouse. She loves music, art, film, and dancing and likes to drink too much gin in the summer and too much scotch in the winter.

Nicholas Kosevich and Ira Koplowitz

For nearly a year before founding Bittercube in 2009, Nicholas and Ira developed the six varieties of Bittercube bitters. The company began macerating larger batches of bitters in July 2010 and now has distribution and wholesale accounts around the country. Beyond bitters, the company has consulted with a number of restaurants and bars, creating unique cocktail programs, and has lent its cocktail prowess to trade shows. It has put on speakeasy events, guest bartending nights, and cocktail dinners around the Midwest. Bittercube has been featured in *Imbibe*, *Timeout*, the *Milwaukee Journal-Sentinel*, *Daily Candy*, and *Mpls.St.Paul Magazine* and on NPR.

Collin Lace

Collin is the head bartender at the Dakota Jazz Club and Restaurant, in charge of the bar's daily operations and the creation of specialty cocktails for national performances.

Chad Larson

Chad started bartending in the mid-1990s but mainly ran kitchens until 2001. After working at large chain bars, he became a corporate bar trainer for Copeland's of New Orleans. Working in New Orleans's French Quarter, he developed a taste for classic cocktails and absorbed as much as he could. He decided to hone his craft and learn about the history and techniques of cock-

Ira Koplowitz, left, and Nicholas
Kosevich (photo by Dan Bishop)

Collin Lace (photo.
Kristen Mors Photography)

Chad Larson

tail making. At Town Talk Diner and Prairie Ale House, he picked up the technical aspects and history of bartending from his peers and read countless vintage cocktail books. He is currently the bar manager at Barrio in St. Paul's Lowertown. Chad won the Twin Cities leg of Bombay Sapphire's Most Inspired Bartender competition in 2011.

Tim Leary

Tim began bartending at the age of seven in his grandparents' basement back-room bar the Teal Room. This Chicago South Side establishment was home to a bar that put others to shame. How he was ever put behind the stick there, serving his cousins pop, remains a mystery. His first legal job was also in a bar, and he wouldn't have it any other way. Tim prides himself on service and a commitment to his guests' enjoyment and currently puts that ethic to work at La Belle Vie.

Garrett Nitzchke

Garrett has worked as a bartender at King & I Thai, the Local, and Psycho Suzi's.

Dan Oskey

Dan resides behind the bar at the Strip Club Meat & Fish in St. Paul. He is a cofounder of Joia Soda and lives in Minneapolis.

Michael Rasmussen

Michael is Johnny's right-hand man at La Belle Vie, which remains the only job from which he has never been fired. He has gone from third-string developmental quarterback to all-pro in his four years there.

Tim Leary

Garrett Nitzchke

Dan Oskey

Richy Rivera

Richy's excitement for nightlife and bartending can be traced to his native Puerto Rico, where he grew up helping his father with the family business. He has been bartending in Minneapolis for the last fifteen years and has worked in a wide range of venues, from nightclubs, pool halls, and pubs to fine-dining restaurants. He can currently be found at Eli's Food and Cocktails in downtown Minneapolis, where he is in charge of the beverage program and invents new and elegant cocktails. Among his many inspirations is the changing weekly menu by executive chef Jeff Weber. Richy has been involved in several local bartending competitions and has been featured in local media and publications.

Christa Robinson

Coming out of the Loring's kitchen back in the mid-1990s, Christa has had the privilege of working with some of the best chefs in Minneapolis. When she made the switch from cook to bartender, her focus was on start-to-finish drink making. Her cocktails have been featured and can often still be found on menus at Rainbow Chinese, King & I Thai, Fabulous Catering, and the Red Stag. She has always believed that a drink should be presented with as much care as a chef's plating and that what goes in the glass should be simple, flavorful, and deliberate.

Jeff Rogers

Jeff has been working behind the stick for fifteen years, in cocktail bars, nightclubs, beach bars, and everything in between. He can make a great traditional cocktail or conjure up something specifically tailored to your taste buds. His experiences have allowed him to travel around the world. Now working for the Blue Plate Restaurant Company, he has guests imbibing at the Lowry, located in Minneapolis's Uptown.

Michael Rasmussen

Richy Rivera

Christa Robinson

Sonya Runkle

Sonya has bartended at King & I Thai, Trader Vic's in San Francisco, Bradstreet Craftshouse, and Psycho Suzi's.

Peder Schweigert

A Minnesota native, Peder moved to the Twin Cities in 2009 after a whirlwind culinary education. He received a grand diploma in culinary arts from the French Culinary Institute in New York City. In New York, Peder was also able to spend six months cooking under Chef Grant Achatz at Alinea, the United States' only three-star Michelin restaurant. Upon his return to the Twin Cities, Peder worked at Town Talk Diner in Minneapolis and Heartland in St. Paul, both known for their innovative cocktails and house-made ingredients. Currently, Peder can be found at Marvel Bar, where he continues taking pride in his house-made vermouths, ginger beer, liqueurs, and cordials.

Thea Sheffert

Thea works at Ciao Bella in Bloomington, Minnesota, and won Bombay Sapphire's first Minneapolis competition in 2007.

Geoffrey Trelstad

Geoffrey has been bartending for over twenty-five years at Minneapolis favorites such as King & I Thai, the legendary Uptown Bar, and Goodfellow's.

Jeff Rogers

Peder Schweigert

Geoffrey Trelstad

Andy Truskolaski
Born in St. Paul, Andy has spent his professional life in the hospitality and food service indus-
tries. He quickly developed a passion for food and drink and has an avid interest in wine and
handcrafted cocktails. He has worked at the Westin Minneapolis since its April 2007 opening,
overseeing the bar for the highly acclaimed restaurant BANK. Andy won the Twin Cities leg of
Bombay Sapphire's Most Inspired Bartender competition in 2010.

216

Andy Truskolaski

Glassware Glossary

 martini glass

martini glass: 6 to 7 ounces; standard, sometimes big, v-shaped glasses

mini-martini glass: 2 ounces

coupe martini or champagne coupe: usually 5 to 6 ounces, a smaller, curvaceous martini-style glass

 sidecar

 champagne coup

sidecar: sometimes served with champagne coupe drinks, to hold excess cocktail; often metal, similar to a small cobbler shaker

mini-collins glass: 7 ounces, small and straight sided; home bartenders might use a juice glass or a smaller (8-ounce) highball

 mini collins glass

 tall collins glass

collins glass: 10 to 14 ounces

tall collins glass: 16 ounces

highball glass: 10 to 12 ounces; sometimes interchangeable with collins glasses

 rocks glass

rocks glass: 6 to 9 ounces; also called old-fashioned glasses

double rocks glass: 10 to 13 ounces; also called double old-fashioned glasses

single shot glass: 1½ ounces

shot glass

double shot glass: 2 to 4 ounces

champagne flute: 6 to 7 ounces

 champagne flute

burgundy wineglass

burgundy wineglass: big and bulbous red wine glass

bordeaux wineglass: red wine glass, more slender than a
  burgundy glass

bordeaux wineglass

white wine glass

white wine glass: smaller than a red wine glass, these have a
  more tapered bowl and a narrower mouth

hurricane glass: 16 to 20 ounces; shaped like a hurricane lamp

sour glass: 5 to 6 ounces; short stem and tulip-shaped bowl; also
  known as a whiskey sour glass

hurricane glass

Acknowledgments

Before saying good-bye, I want to thank you for buying this book. All royalties will go to support SPCA International, and I hope it will raise a lot of money for this compassionate and forward-thinking organization. I also want to thank my fellow North Star Bartenders' Guild members for so generously contributing their original recipes. I hope they inspire you to re-create some of these cocktails at home—or to create your own originals based on ideas born from them.

Photographer Kate Sommers gets a gold star for taking over six hundred pictures on cocktail photo day, as well as for indulging my request to snap a photo of me at home with my gargoyle. Tim McKee and Bill Summerville: thank you for hiring me and giving me the freedom to do my thing. I don't think there's another James Beard Award–winning restaurant in the country that would've let me off the leash like you guys have. I still laugh when I recall the time I gave the office manager a new drink to add to the list—Put Your Ray Gun to My Head (a David Bowie lyric)—and she didn't even blink.

But most of all, I want to thank the whole team at the Minnesota Historical Society Press/Borealis Books. Like I said before, I never aspired to write a cocktail book, but when they asked, I couldn't say no. I'm also pretty sure they got way more than they bargained for (and anyone who knows me knows exactly what I'm talking about and is probably laughing right now). They all deserve medals for saintly patience. I just want to thank them sincerely for putting up with me.

Well, I guess that's it. Hope to see you soon.

Johnny Michaels

North Star Cocktails is set in the Goudy Old Style typeface family. Book design by Jim Davis of Mind*Spark Creative. Typesetting and design by Allan S. Johnson, Phoenix Type, Inc., Appleton, Minnesota.